Children
of
Alcoholics/Addicts

The Author

Richard L. Towers is Director, Department of Alternative and Supplementary Education, Montgomery County Public Schools, Maryland. He is also the author of *How Schools Can Help Combat Student Drug and Alcohol Abuse*, published by NEA.

The Advisory Panel

Sheri Bauman, Counselor, Centennial Adult High School, Fort Collins, Colorado

Richard Culyer, Professor of Education, Coker College, Hartsville, South Carolina

Rita K. Gram, Elementary School Counselor, University City School District, Missouri

David N. Wallace, Social Studies Teacher, Lebanon High School, Lebanon, New Hampshire

Allen R. Warner, Assistant Dean, College of Education, University of Houston, Texas

Children
of
Alcoholics/Addicts

by Richard L. Towers

with a Workshop Leader's Guide
by Rita Rumbaugh

nea PROFESSIONAL LIBRARY
National Education Association
Washington, D.C.

For childen of alcoholics/addicts
of all ages

Copyright © 1989
National Education Association of the United States

Printing History
    First Printing: September 1989

Note

The opinions expressed in this publication should not be construed as represent-
ing the policy or position of the National Education Association. Materials published by the NEA Professional Library are intended to be discussion documents
for educators who are concerned with specialized interests of the profession.

Library of Congress Cataloging-in-Publication Data

Towers, Richard L.
        Children of alcoholics/addicts/Richard L. Towers; with a
workshop leader's guide by Rita Rumbaugh.
                p.   cm.   (At-risk series)
        Bibliography: p.
        ISBN 0-8106-0242-3
        1. Children of alcoholics—Counseling of—United States.
        2. Children of narcotic addicts—Counseling—United States.
        I. Rumbaugh, Rita. II. Title. III. Series.
HV5132.T68   1986
362.29 13 0973—dc20   89-35491
                                                                CIP

CONTENTS

1. INTRODUCTION

A little more than 20 years ago, the Wilson kids... were normal and happy. A year ago, Michael tried to kill himself. Danny has shot cocaine. Chris has done so many drugs that those who love him fear half his brain is burned away. Tena's the lucky one. She got out. She... is married and has recently had a second child. She's the one with the purpose in life, the one said to be free of emotional ravage. But all you need to do is spend an evening with her and sentences like this will start to drop hard: "I was always terrified when I was a teenager of coming home and finding my three brothers dead. I mean, not just dead, but carved up into a hundred little pieces. By my father." And yet Tena, second eldest, 27, free of drugs, will also say this: "Listen, I know my parents smoked pot and had parties and... were experimenting with some other things when we were growing up. What's so unusual about that in the 60's and 70's?"

—Paul Hendrickson,"Nightmare on Black Rock Road." Washington Post Magazine, December 11, 1988.

The list of factors that put students at high risk of failing in school and in life is a long one (see Appendix C). It includes poor basic skills, low self-esteem, chronic truancy, eating disorders, sexual promiscuity/pregnancy, delinquent behavior, drug abuse, and dropping out of school. Living in a household where drugs and/or alcohol are chronically abused is a factor that is less frequently mentioned; and yet it puts millions of children at extreme risk of failure in school and/or life, and may be behind many of the other risk factors.

The consequences of drug and alcohol abuse for our nation and for our children have been well documented. They undermine our economy, threaten public safety and security, and threaten our lives. To those of us who work with troubled children and youths, it comes as no surprise that family conditions are intertwined with student problems. The diseases of alcoholism and drug addiction are good examples because persons living in a family with an alcoholic or addict can be as adversely affected by the disease as the substance abuser.

Alcoholics and drug addicts hurt those around them by destroying family stability, unity, and security. At its worst, alcoholism/addiction can result in loss of income and self-respect, spousal and child abuse, and divorce. For the children, it can lead to delinquency, substance abuse, and suicide. At the least, children of alcoholics/addicts will suffer feelings of low self-esteem, shame, fear, and loneliness; and they may grow up lacking in the ability to trust and develop relationships with others. It will certainly affect how well or poorly they function in school.

Estimates of how many children of alcoholics (COAs) there are in the United States vary from 6 million to 65 million (1).* Estimates of the number of COAs under the age of 18 range from 7 million to 15 million. This amounts to between 4 and 6 such children in a classroom of 25 (2). Add to this the children growing up in families where other drugs are abused regularly, either by parents or siblings, and that number increases significantly. The disease is no respecter of class or position. It affects all income levels, races, sexes, and geographic locations. The public admission of problems with alcohol and drugs by prominent Americans such as First Lady Betty Ford and others has helped bring it "out of the closet."

Although we frequently use the terms "alcoholic" and "disease," it should be noted that experts disagree widely over the definition of these terms. For our purposes the terms "alcoholism," "problem drinking," and "alcohol dependence" are used interchangeably, as are the words "alcoholic" and "addict." Our focus is on the child and the effects on that child of growing up in a family where severe, chronic abuse of a chemical substance, be it alcohol or amphetamines, occurs. Terms such as "children of alcoholics" (COAs) "children of substance abusers" (COSAs), "children of alcoholics/addicts," and "children whose parents are chemically dependent" are used interchangeably in this publication. Although we do recognize differences among chemical substances, our definition of alcoholism/addiction, like that of the DSM IIIR *(Diagnostic and Statistical Manual of Mental Disorders* of the American Psychiatric Association, 3d rev. ed., May 1987), focuses on the commonalities of physiological tolerance: occupational, social, and familial dysfunction; inability to abstain; and possible physical damage, as well as the progressive nature of the disease (3).

Fortunately, support groups such as Alcoholics Anonymous (AA) and Narcotics Anonymous (NA) (for alcoholics/addicts), Adult Children of Alcoholics (ACOA), Al-Anon (for spouses and other family members), and Alateen (for teenage children) exist to help those in need. But support for the younger children of alcoholics and addicts continues to be a serious gap in the continuum of care for those affected by this disease; and only a small percentage of children whose parents are chemically dependent receive the help they need (4). It is important, therefore, that school personnel understand how parental alcoholism and drug addiction affect the lives of their students. It is important that we understand

---

*Numbers in parentheses appearing in the text refer to the Notes beginning on page 75.

addictive disease; if we don't understand the disease, we cannot hope to understand how it affects our students. The time when schools can deal only with the three Rs is long gone. If children are not available for instruction, we cannot teach them effectively or otherwise; and the children of alcoholics/addicts frequently are not available for instruction.

Over the past decade, we have seen a significant decline in the number of in-school students who regularly abuse drugs. Even the number of students using cocaine and crack, which was of epidemic proportions has declined for the second year in a row (according to data collected in 1988, by the University of Michigan) (5). Use by students of the most abused drug of all, alcohol, likewise has declined. Student abuse of drugs and alcohol remains a major problem, but progress has been made. Notwithstanding the pessimism of the media, there are success stories. Schools have worked hard with police, health departments, social service agencies, and parents in getting the antidrug message across; and it has had an effect, despite the current surge in drug-related violence and increased drug use in some subgroups of the population. This effort by schools must be sustained; and other organizations that have more recently joined with us in concrete ways must stay with it—big business, the entertainment industry, professional sports, religion, and the national government.

More attention, however, must be given to the influence of the family. A new phenomenon of the past few years is the emergence of organized activity by, and increased awareness of, adult children of alcoholics. This, in turn, has drawn attention to the importance of working with young children and teens whose parents are chemically dependent, and to the critical importance of the effect of the family on high-risk youth. New program approaches—focusing on ways to strengthen family functioning, relationships, and parenting practices—are receiving much-needed funding from the U.S. Office of Substance Abuse Prevention. Many of these approaches are based on research showing that "chronic family discord and turbulence are associated with juvenile delinquency and other negative consequences for vulnerable children..." and that "positive parent-child relationships and structure and rules in the household seem to protect vulnerable children" (5a). This development can only help in our fight against drug and alcohol abuse, and deserves our attention, support, and involvement.

The environmental factors that may cause young people to abuse drugs have long been linked to a lackadaisical or permissive attitude in the family toward drugs or alcohol. Add to this the lack of structure, failure to develop appropriate coping skills, fears and anxieties, poor self-image, and a possible genetic predisposition, and the chances of using

9

and becoming addicted to alcohol or drugs are very great for a child or youth in a substance-abusing family.

The purpose of this publication is to raise the awareness of teachers and other school personnel to the needs and characteristics of the children of alcoholics and addicts and to explain what schools can do to help. In the following pages we will explain—

- why school personnel should be concerned;
- how the disease of alcoholism and addiction develops, progresses, and affects the family;
- what the impact of this experience is on the children who come from these homes;
- how to identify these children;
- what to do, both within the classroom and outside of it, to help these children; and
- where to go for information, materials, and help.

It may seem that we paint a gloomy picture of the future for children of alcoholics/addicts. The issues they must deal with and the risks they run may seem insurmountable We describe these in the pages that follow because it's important for teachers and other school personnel to have an understanding of parental alcoholism/addiction and what it can mean for the children they teach. We do not mean to suggest, however, that there is no hope, or that COAs must inevitably be relegated to the status of afflicted, unfortunate people. Many COAs have risen above the risk factors to become healthy, happy, and successful people. Indeed, people who get help and spend time learning to understand and cope with the disease and its ramifications (as with the 12 Steps of AA), often develop insights and strengths in excess of those who have had no adversity to overcome and have not taken the time and made the considerable effort to understand and work through their problems.

Note also that although this publication speaks mostly of alcohol addiction, much of what is said here also applies to dependence on other drugs as well—cocaine, heroin, "uppers, downers."

Chapter 6 provides a guide for using this book to conduct a workshop for faculty and staff. The publication also may be used with parents and others who support the efforts of schools to meet the needs of all the children whose lives we touch.

For the most part, the information, resources, and reflections presented are a summary of the best thinking and experience of experts in the field. We have culled from a variety of sources what we feel is most useful for school personnel. For those who wish to go directly to the primary and secondary sources, documentation and references are included.

2. THE RISKS

There's alcoholism all through my family. My grandmother and three of my aunts drank themselves to death. Now my brother drinks like a fish. He and my cousin got me started drinking.

—Ellen, age 16

The children of alcoholics and/or drug-addicted parents run many risks. They are at substantially higher risk (one in four) of becoming substance abusers themselves than children and youths whose parents do not abuse drugs and alcohol (6). They have greater socialization problems, and are more likely to be suspended from school and to run away from home (7). Most of these children and adolescents suffer from low self-esteem and the adolescents often display poor social judgment (8). As adults they are more likely to have failed marriages and to be unsuccessful at work and in supporting themselves and their families (9).

RISK FACTORS

Adults who abuse alcohol and drugs tend not to make good parents. Mothers who drink and/or use drugs during pregnancy expose their babies to risks of mental retardation and a variety of physical problems (10). Alcohol and drug use by parents also has been linked to physical and sexual abuse and is most certainly a cause of child neglect (11). Alcoholism/addiction in a home goes hand in hand with physical violence and abuse in the home. COAs may be battered by the alcoholic parent, the nonalcoholic parent, or by the male or female companion of either in cases where the parents are divorced or separated. Sometimes COAs will develop the same denial of the abuse and battery as they do of the drinking that goes on in the home (12).

The alcoholic parent becomes increasingly dysfunctional and has difficulty in maintaining a responsible role as spouse, parent, or employee. Meals may not be made, report cards or field trip permission slips may not be signed, bills may not be paid nor lunch money given to the child, and arguments between parents—and even violence—may occur in the home (13). These factors coupled with the parents' unpredictable behavior can promote instability and hopelessness in children (14). Often, inappropriate roles such as preparing meals, cleaning the house, and even paying bills and taking care of younger siblings are thrust prematurely on these children. Poor attendance, poor academic performance, and acting-out behavior in school may result (15).

11

PSYCHOLOGICAL, EMOTIONAL, AND DEVELOPMENTAL CONSEQUENCES

Since much of their lives may be involved in keeping the alcoholism/addiction in their family a secret rather than in getting help to deal with it, children of alcoholics/addicts tend not to develop relationships where they can confide in and trust others (16). The resulting psychological and physical stress of living in a dysfunctional family can also produce physical ailments in the child that may go unattended because the family's focus is on the effects of the drinking or drugging behavior of the parent. Preoccupation with what is happening in the home may also distract children from concentrating in school and completing homework at home (17).

> That's just how our family is. We just don't talk about what goes on at home even among ourselves and certainly not to others. It's just not their business. No one ever told me not to talk about it to anyone. It's just something I picked up on.
>
> —Ronnie, age 14

It's important to note that parental alcohol or drug dependence does not lead to the same outcomes in every case. A number of variables bear on how a child is affected (18). Younger children, for example, are more likely than older ones to experience damaging outcomes, particularly if the parent's chemical dependence is at an advanced stage. This is true both in terms of physical problems associated with the pregnancy and developmental problems associated with a basic need of newborns for consistent parenting that builds trust in the self and in human relationships (19). These children have more severe social and psychological problems in later life than those who first encounter parental alcoholism/addiction in adolescence (20). Similarly, the accomplishment of developmental tasks that children need to complete as toddlers and during the years prior to entering kindergarten or first grade may be impeded by an alcoholic mother or by living in a home preoccupied with a parent's substance abuse. For example, a child who is confined in a playpen for hours on end to "get him or her out of mom's hair" will not be able to exercise the natural curiosity or develop the autonomy, intelligence, and confidence that will be needed when he or she begins school (21). Such children also may have greater difficulty in separating from parents in kindergarten and first grade and may throw tantrums (22).

The development of a child's trust in parents and in the world usually

12

occurs in the first five years of life. In alcholic and drug-abusing families, because of the parents' erratic behavior, this trust is not always normally developed (23). COAs may learn to mistrust and/or not learn to differentiate between their own misdeeds and those of someone else when they are punished or abused. COAs may learn that they cannot trust anyone to take care of them. Indeed, since parental and children's roles are often reversed, such youngsters may grow up unsure of who is taking care of whom. Because children of this age are so vulnerable to shame, they often believe that there is something wrong with them (24). The alcoholic or drug abuser whose life, job, and marriage is not going well will often blame others, including the children, for his or her feelings of failure (25). Children 0 to 5 years of age in an alcoholic or drug-dependent family, therefore, may not have the atmosphere of trust and security that they require to develop appropriately (26).

Children may come to school at age 5 or 6; therefore, if they come from a substance-abusing environment they are at risk for failure before they even begin school. On the other hand, a bright child in an alcoholic family may gain a great deal from school, finding it a welcome opportunity to build self-esteem and to profit from the structure, discipline, and stimulation that is lacking at home (27). Unfortunately, COAs may just as easily go in the opposite direction. The point is, not all children of chemically dependent parents are alike, and they will respond to school differently.

At ages 6 to 11, children tend to see themselves in terms of how their parents view them (28). At this age they crave attention. If they don't receive it, they feel rejected and unimportant. This is the stage of "concrete operations," when children view the world as black and white and have not yet begun to think abstractly (29).

A child's life focus remains with the family, even during early adolescence (up to about 13 years of age) (30). During middle adolescence (14 through 16 years of age), revolt against parental authority and conformance to peer group standards begins for most (31). As adolescents, children of alcoholics have a greater tendency for adjustment problems (32). During late adolescence (17 to 19 years of age), the ability to begin to make decisions and to get ready for the future depends, according to Erikson, on "successfully integrating past developmental stages and developing an ego identity" (33). By this time, most teens have experimented with alcohol and many have tried other drugs. Those most vulnerable to the risk of advancing from experimentation to drug abuse and dependence are the children of substance abusers (34).

In an alcoholic or a drug-abusing family, children may develop the sense that they are worthless. They get no attention at home because the

13

focus is on the addict in the family; thus, they feel rejected and unimportant. What's more, they may feel responsible for the parent's substance abuse and obligated to look after him or her—just at a time when they should be getting ready to withdraw from the family, exercise more independence, and enter into outside relationships, especially with the opposite sex (35). The result is a feeling of guilt and, for some, alienation from the larger society (36). Many of these youngsters learn manipulative behaviors to get their needs met.

Social isolation also may interfere with developing peer relationships and with the emotional support derived from peer groups; thus, the youngster may feel hopeless, fearful, and lonely (37). If word gets around among other parents that a child lives in an alcoholic home, they probably will direct their children not to associate with that child (38). This can lead COAs to succumb to pressures to use drugs in an effort to be accepted by a peer group—any peer group.

> Children of alcoholics are people who have been robbed of their childhood.
>
> —*Newsweek*

PROBLEMS CAUSED BY PARENTAL SUBSTANCE ABUSE

The following are some typical problems for children resulting from a parent's alcoholism or drug addiction (39):

- *Guilt,* when the child begins to believe the addict's accusations that he or she is responsible for the drinking or drug taking.
- *Shame* for the parent, which can cause withdrawal from friends, not wanting to invite anybody home after school. (Often the child will become a coconspirator and try to hide the drug or drinking problem from outsiders.)
- *Resentment* of the alcoholic or drug-abusing parent. (The child may begin to resent not having a normal life or the violence that may occur between parents, or between siblings and parents. Children may lose respect for the nonchemically dependent parent for not taking a stronger stand to prevent the problem.)
- *Fear* that he or she will be physically harmed by the parent who is under the influence of drugs or alcohol, or that the substance-abusing parent may die in an accident while driving a car, or in some other manner while under the influence of drugs or alcohol.

14

- *Insecurity,* particularly when an alcoholic or drug-addicted parent becomes unpredictable or neglectful of the family's physical and emotional needs. (Parents who are addicted to drugs or alcohol as well as nonaddicted spouses may have little time for other family members. The nonaddicted spouse may be too busy covering up for, and picking up the pieces after, the drug- or alcohol-addicted spouse.)
- *Delinquency* by children who are frustrated and unable to deal with the stress of an alcoholic or drug-centered home. (Such children may react aggressively and in destructive ways.)
- *Financial troubles.* (Drug abuse and alcoholism almost always affect job security and financial stability. In addition, the cost of supplying the abuser with alcohol and drugs can be substantial, using up the money that the family may need for food, clothes, or housing.)

Children who grow up in homes where alcohol and drugs are abused are at risk of developing physical, developmental, and/or psychological problems that may surface in school as attention-deficit disorders; in law enforcement agencies as child abuse, incest, or neglect; or at doctors' offices as fetal alcohol syndrome or other alcohol-related birth defects.

Some people were quoted in the *Washington Post*, January 2, 1989, on the impact drugs have had on them.

"They were freebasing crack on the front porch of the house next door. A fire started and burned their home and my front porch down."
—a Northeast Washington woman, age 32

"My daughter is 26, and she is on drugs real bad. She has a 10-year-old son that I keep. She can't take care of him. I got her in a program. She got out and isn't any better. Last week she got him from me and, I think, had him selling drugs."
—a Southeast Washington woman, age 54

"My neighbor was about to lose his home because he was buying drugs with his mortgage money."
"—a Capitol Heights woman, age 31

"We came home and found my oldest son unconscious in the bathroom with a needle in his arm. My granddaughter found him."
"—a Northeast Washington woman, age 55

CHARACTERISTICS OF AT-RISK CHILDREN

In general, then, children of alcoholics/addicts who live in dysfunctional families often exhibit specific characteristics that place them at risk. Metzger has completed a list of such characteristics from a review of the literature (40):

- Difficulty in creating and maintaining trusting relationships, often leading to isolation. (This is caused by inconsistent and unpredictable parental behavior.)
- Low self-esteem, which may be a result of parental insecurities and inconsistent parental expectations.
- Self-doubt, particularly about one's own judgment and perception, sometimes making the child dependent on others for guidance and hesitant to make a decision.
- Difficulty in being spontaneous and open, caused by a need to be in control and to minimize the risk of being surprised. (This may be a reaction to living in a chaotic household where the child is at the mercy of others.)
- Denial and repression, which become second nature and are displayed as central personality traits because of the need to collaborate with other family members in keeping "the secret."
- General feelings of guilt about a number of areas for which the child had no responsibility. (This may be a result of the child's guilt feelings about the parent's drinking, for which the child may have inappropriately assumed responsibility.)
- An uncertainty about his or her own feelings and desires caused by shifting parental roles as the chemically dependent parent's addiction progresses.
- Seeing things in an "all or nothing" context, which sometimes manifests itself in a perfectionist fear of failure.
- Poor impulse control, which may result in acting-out behavior in school and elsewhere, probably caused by a lack of appropriate parental guidance, love, and discipline.
- A potential for psychiatric illnesses such as depression, phobias, panic reactions, and hyperactivity.
- A preoccupation with the family and failure to leave home caused by the youth seeing himself/herself as being needed and responsible for taking care of the family or parent.
- Abuse of alcohol and/or drugs either because of a genetic predisposition and/or because of parental modeling.

16

In school, these characteristics may affect students' abilities to concentrate and hence learn, their attitude toward and relationship with teachers and others in authority as well as with their peers, their classroom behavior, their attendance, whether they complete homework assignments, their participation in extracurricular activities and sports—in short, just about all aspects of their schooling.

3. HOW SCHOOLS ARE AFFECTED

My mom and stepdad separated five times from the time I was in grade 3 to grade 5. Stuff is always breaking in our house and being thrown. It makes me nervous. Even in school.

—Butch, age 13

Schools have never been able to immunize themselves from the problems of the larger society. Like it or not, we are affected by what goes on outside our walls—poverty, violence, racism, drug and alcohol abuse, and the dissolution of the family are only a few of the forces gnawing at our ability to educate America's young. Parental, and even sibling drug and alcohol abuse also have a significant effect on schools. Whatever affects our students affects our ability to do our job. Problems at home invariably manifest themselves in school. An Al-Anon and Alateen motto says it all: "You don't have to drink to suffer from alcoholism."

Within a family where there is alcoholism and/or drug addiction, relationships are almost always strained, resulting in anxiety and depression (41). Children who come to school angry and depressed are not only unavailable for instruction themselves, but also make it difficult for others to learn and for teachers to teach.

PARENTAL NEGLECT

Among the special problems of children of substance abusers, which include hyperactivity, bed-wetting, and suicide, several that relate even more directly to how they do in school have been documented (42). For example, in addition to being at risk for physical and sexual abuse, children of alcoholics/addicts typically are victims of child neglect and, in particular, of educational neglect. This kind of neglect takes the form of a lack of interest on the part of the parents in how well, or how poorly, the child is doing in school, or even whether the child attends school. When other students' parents have signed their report cards or sent in grandma's recipe for the "family traditions" unit in social studies, or come to see their child perform in the PTA's holiday musicale, this child's parents rarely follow through on time, if at all. If the parent does show up at the PTA or for a teacher/parent conference, it's likely to be a

18

stressful and embarrassing experience for the child, who can never be sure in what condition the parent will appear. Even the non-alcoholic/addicted parent, who often is preoccupied with how to deal with (or cover up) the spouse's problem, or with his or her own anxiety and depression, will have little time or attention to devote to the child's school activities.

Most parents, chemically dependent ones included, love their children and want what is best for them. But parents, particularly chemically dependent ones and their spouses, may not always do what is best for their children. In NEA's *How Schools Can Help Combat Student Drug and Alcohol Abuse*, teachers are urged, when they become aware of student drug or alcohol abuse, among other things, to notify the parents of their concerns. If this call from the school comes to an alcoholic/addict or to a spouse who is in a state of denial, it is likely to be met with hostility and denial. Because admitting that drug or alcohol use may be harmful for the student could mean a similar acknowledgment for oneself, the parent probably will resist facing the truth until very serious consequences have befallen the youth. This denial may result in the parent's failure to follow through on treatment or referral recommendations from the school. Additionally, parents who feel guilty about their own or their spouse's drinking or drug use frequently either minimize or fail to acknowledge altogether any family problems when speaking with a teacher, counselor, or administrator who is trying to figure out how to help a troubled and/or troublesome student.

> My Mom is a great enabler. Like if I failed a subject or get detention, my Mom would like say, "Don't tell your Dad." He never saw any of my report cards from 3rd to 6th grade. My Mom always had an excuse why he drank. Like he's tired; he's under stress at work, etc. She'd always cover up for him.
>
> —Mark, age 17

COGNITIVE AND EMOTIONAL FACTORS

In a recent study of problems among school-age children of alcoholic parents, significant differences were found in emotional and cognitive factors including self-concept, emotional disorder, and intelligence between children with alcoholic parents and those with nonalcoholic parents (43). Behavioral differences, including psychosomatic symptoms and hyperactive behavior, also showed a trend toward significance. It just

19

stands to reason that children who don't sleep well because of fear and anxiety or who stay up late taking care of siblings or parents will be tired in school the next day. Kids who are tired, distracted, fearful, and preoccupied will not do well.

It has been theorized that lower cognitive and emotional functioning among children of alcoholics/addicts may be the result of the alcoholic family's being generally less successful than the nonalcoholic family in establishing a well-planned, stable, and meaningful family life (44).

The mood swings or emotional extremes that Wilmes discusses, and which can be observed in the classroom among various children, can range from rage to depression, with everything in between, such as anger, anxiety, interest, calm, relaxation, disinterest, or boredom (45). Usually these mood swings on the part of the child reflect the mood swings of the alcoholic parent (46). In other words, the child in a substance-abusing family generally internalizes the mood swings into his/her daily living pattern.

Such a child may also develop a love/hate relationship with his/her family, partly as a result of the extreme nature of the moods within the family (47). Sometimes the child will be preoccupied with hate thoughts toward the family. At the same time, the child is dependent on the family. The natural outcome of unpredictable mood swings is the general feeling of uncertainty (48). This makes children of alcohol/drug abusers preoccupied and fearful about the future and about what will become of them, and can account for insecurity and anxiety in the child. "Will Mom fall, hit her head and die while she's on a binge? Has Dad had another auto accident? He should've been home by now. Will he be drunk when he gets home, and beat Mom and Sis?"

Consider, for example, the child who witnesses extreme and violent arguments over the dinner table each evening. This child will begin associating tension and fear with family get-togethers. While the rest of the class may look forward to talking about, learning about, and participating in holiday activities, the child of a chemically dependent parent may become very anxious at the prospect of a family get-together at Thanksgiving or Christmas; and this may be reflected in his/her attitude toward holiday-related school activities.

In school, particularly elementary school, where holiday celebrations often are incorporated into academics and other activities, such children will be moody, withdrawn, irritable, and certainly not ready or able to participate with the rest of the class and the teacher in holiday-related lessons and activities. At such times, these children may become disruptive and abusive toward the teacher and other children. Older children may experience such severe depression and anxiety at these times of the

20

year that they become susceptible to self-destructive behavior such as drug/alcohol use and even suicide.

> I always promised myself I'd never be like him but when I used, I was exactly like him.
>
> —Angie, age 16

Whitfield has estimated that 80 percent of all adolescent suicides are children of alcoholics (49). This may be too high an estimate. Certainly, the majority of adolescent suicides and suicide attempts involve the use of drugs or alcohol and it has been clearly established that there is a high incidence of alcohol and drug abuse by adolescents whose parents abuse these substances (50). Wilmes points out that most studies of children of alcoholics show a trend toward social skills problems as many of these children have minimal opportunity for social development within the home (51). This may be accounted for by the fact that alcohol- and drug-abusing parents usually socialize outside the home (especially when the alcoholic is male) and the child is often afraid to bring friends home from school lest he or she be embarrassed by arguments or displays of inebriation in front of friends. The consequence is that the child of the alcoholic typically has problems in developing peer relationships or making friends (52). These children often are alienated and isolated from other children. Isolation and alienation may also extend to their relationship with their teachers. Classroom methodology that requires student teaming such as cooperative education will need to make accommodations for these children.

Because children often feel responsible for their parents' behavior (witness the guilt feelings when parent divorce), children of alcohol/drug abusers, in particular, may feel that if they had done better in school or not misbehaved at home, home problems would not have occurred. Feelings of guilt and resentment are common in children of alcohol/drug abusers; these emotions are observed in children at almost all ages, even among the very young who may not realize what they are experiencing or feeling (53). A number of authors have reported on the ways children deal with this reaction, such as acting-out behavior and withdrawal (54). But some children may be motivated to do very well in school. These overachievers may feel this is the only way they can compensate for what they perceive to be their guilt in causing the problem at home. And so they will pull out all the stops to do well in an effort to somehow make up for their perceived role in their parents' substance abuse.

21

This may not appear to be a problem until you stop to realize that any compulsion, even one to do well in school, can be unhealthy. In this situation, a child who wants desperately to do well and perhaps make expiation for any responsibility—real or imagined—for the parent's problem, may react irrationally if he/she does poorly on a test or in a course. Such a child may become violent or may even try to take his/her life. A child's contemplation of suicide can be serious. Most school districts have policies urging staff to take all threats and symptoms of suicidal ideation very seriously. Usually, this includes immediately notifying a mental health professional at the school as well as the parents. For children of chemically dependent parents, however, the assumption cannot always be made that the ideation or threat of suicide will be attended to responsibly by parents. Schools, therefore, when warranted, should make additional arrangements in the case of COAs, such as involving the child protection team of the local social services agency.

In a survey by Margaret Cork, 125 children of alcoholics indicated the ways in which they were affected by their parents' alcohol abuse (55). These effects ranged from feeling uncomfortable with the opposite sex [48] to not being able to trust others [31]. One hundred and eight of the children felt that their self-confidence was affected in that they never felt sure of themselves, and 112 said that they felt unwanted by one or both parents, while 111 thought their relationships with persons outside of the family were also affected.

It's frightening because I have a bad temper and my Dad has a bad temper and we used to get into fights. He always knew what to say to hurt me. I was always in a bad mood.

—Sandy, age 15

As educators, we understand the importance of self-concept to educational attainment and how difficult it is to help youngsters who feel unwanted and insecure to have the confidence to take the risks necessary to learn. These children, in particular, need positive attention and focused time from an adult. Teachers whom they can rely on to be fair and consistent over an extended period can help restore their trust in adults.

4. A FAMILY DISEASE

I decided that this disease took the first half of my life, and goddam it, it wasn't going to take the second half of it.

—Suzanne Somers

Simply stated, an alcoholic is a person who cannot abstain from drinking no matter what the consequences may be. Here we are most concerned with the consequences to children in alcoholic and chemically dependent families. In order to understand and help students who live in such families, it is important that we have some understanding of alcoholism / addiction.

DISEASE THEORY

Alcoholism / addiction is a progressive disease, generally moving on from an experimental / learning phase to a seeking middle phase to a harmful dependency phase requiring more and more of the alcohol or drugs just to feel normal. The disease is chronic or ongoing and characterized by deterioration of physical, social, emotional, and all other aspects of the alcoholic / addict's life. It will continue until it ultimately destroys the person afflicted with it, and may result in death. Unfortunately, it may also result in destroying those around the addict. It will almost certainly impair the health of the family unit. It is in this sense, therefore, that alcoholism / addiction is a family disease—not because it is caused by the family. Seventeen million people from under 9 to over 90 years of age suffer from it; 25 percent of these people are teenagers (56); 40 percent are women (57). Alcoholism / addiction is said to be responsible for over 30 percent of all suicides, 55 percent of all auto fatalities, 60 percent of all child abuse, 65 percent of all drownings, and 85 percent of all home violence (58). Less than 1 in 10 recovers (59). It manifests itself in many ways, and can be as variable as people themselves.

Over the years, there has been a great deal of discussion about whether alcoholism / addiction is a disease. Some people believe it is a character disorder, that the alcoholic / addict is an immoral person who chooses to abuse drugs and / or alcohol because of some flaw or character defect. Others consider it to be a symptom of family dysfunction; and that if the family were functioning appropriately, it would disappear.

23

> I've seen five-year-olds running entire families.
>
> —Janet G. Woititz, COA Associate

Those who subscribe to the disease theory see alcoholism/addiction as a progressive, debilitating condition that is amoral. Like other diseases, it can run in families and may be genetically transmitted. Current theory holds that alcoholism/addiction has a combination of causes, both environmental and biological.

CHARACTERISTICS OF THE DISEASE

In general, the addictive disease is characterized by many of the following elements identified in the 1967 American Medical Association definition (60):

- A preoccupation with the drug or alcohol
- A loss of control over the use of the substance and inability to abstain
- Persistent and excessive use of the substance
- A chronicity, or ongoing dimension to the problem
- A progression, or element of increasing involvement, loss of control, and tolerance
- Impaired emotional, occupational, social, and/or familial health
- A tendency toward relapse
- Physical disability (such as blackouts or impaired cardiovascular functioning).

As the addict/alcoholic progresses from initial to more advanced stages of the illness, more of these elements will appear and the effects on the family will become more and more pronounced. The following behaviors will become common (61):

- Alcoholics and drug addicts will resort to their drug or alcohol to cope with everyday stress, using larger and larger amounts to achieve the desired effect.
- Fear and anxiety will affect them more and more frequently, creating a poor self-image and sometimes violent emotions.
- They will argue over their drinking or drug-taking habits, strenu-

24

ously objecting and denying whenever they are confronted.

- They will make solemn promises to quit using drugs, or to stop drinking, or to drink less, or to change their brand of liquor, or to behave better, if only the spouse will stop "nagging."
- They will progressively ignore and avoid more and more of their responsibilities to their families, their friends, their jobs, their children's school, etc.
- Finally, they will begin to experience "blackouts" more and more often, where they can't remember what happened during a drinking episode.

There are many reasons why people drink and take drugs. What is important for our discussion, however, is that alcoholics and drug addicts do become physically as well as emotionally addicted to the substance they are abusing and come to rely on the alcohol or drug simply in order to function day by day. When this happens, others in the household, particularly children, are adversely affected.

> I always tried to make peace between my Mom and Dad whenever they'd argue. Sometimes I'd purposely get my Dad mad at me so he'd leave my Mom and brother alone.
>
> —Fran, age 14

ENABLING AND CODEPENDENCY

In addition to having excuses (as opposed to reasons) why they drink, alcoholics and drug addicts often enlist children and spouses as enablers and co-conspirators, securing from them not simply their tolerance but their active assistance and encouragement (62). For example, spouses or children often will be asked to cover up for the parent who is too drunk to get out of bed and go to work. They may have to call in with the excuse. A spouse or child may even be asked to obtain the alcohol or drugs for the parent. The nonalcoholic parent may recruit the child to hide the liquor from the alcoholic or other family members, and the alcoholic parent may ask the child to hide it from the nonalcoholic spouse or other family members. A child will often make excuses at school about why a parent cannot come to a parent conference, a PTA meeting, or an athletic event. Sometimes children may have to take on adult roles prematurely, compensating for the abdication of responsibility by the parent. Children and spouses who support the alcoholic/addict's chemical

25

dependence in these ways often are not aware that by shielding the person from the negative consequences of the addiction they're actually harming the person. The Johnson Institute sums it up this way (63):

> "For an alcoholic to continue drinking, nonalcoholics must be unwittingly involved in enabling (that is, encouraging) the alcoholic's drinking" and ... "those close to an alcoholic are inclined to develop behavior and/or emotional problems of their own as they attempt to make adjustments to the ... disease."

In some situations, families can become involved in the abuser's addiction to the extent that they become both enablers and deniers of the problem at the same time. The abuser's problem becomes their problem to the extent that they are called "codependents" and often will protect the abuser by lying, covering up, and actually assuming a role that is dependent on protecting, caring for, and making excuses for the abuser. The codependent usually is a spouse, but often it is a child. Codependents commonly have low self-esteem; therefore, they find meaning in making themselves indispensable to others. They are devoted servers (64). Family members may feel guilty as the abuser's behavior becomes more unmanageable and the addiction grows worse. They may feel that they are somehow responsible for the addict's crisis, and this, in turn, increases their dependency on the addict, which ironically may deter the addict from being motivated to get treatment.

ROLES

Wegscheider has described the various roles that children assume in the classic alcoholic family in an effort to cope with what is happening around them (65). Almost all of the roles serve to help the parent maintain the drug or alcohol habit:

1. *The Caretaker (or Enabler)*. Although this role is generally filled by the spouse, children sometimes enable by helping to take care of, and covering up for the parent. Thus, the alcoholic is kept from suffering the consequences of his/her own actions. As an adult, this child, who often is the oldest sibling, frequently marries an alcoholic. This child, who often is under great stress and in poor health, experiences resentment, embarrassment, and a poor self-image. It never occurs to this child that he/she has any choices other than to do what he/she is doing.

26

2. *The Family Hero.* This child typically is a high achiever outside the home and usually excels in school or in sports, trying to make the parents proud of him/her, hoping that perhaps this will solve the problems at home. This child puts himself/herself under great pressure but is seldom satisfied with his/her accomplishments. This person often becomes a perfectionist and a workaholic and keeps his/her anger and resentment inside. He/she has problems being open, trusting, and loving, and can't seem to form a good relationship. As an adult, this person's marriage frequently ends in divorce.

3. *The Lost Child.* This child reacts to family tension by withdrawing. He/she often is a younger sibling who enters the family when the addiction/alcoholism is at its worst. This child develops problems with depression, loneliness, and alienation. His/her withdrawal becomes a lifelong pattern. This child rarely uses his/her ability and may not learn to read. This child often retreats into a fantasy world, becoming a candidate for mental illness. However, he/she almost never causes trouble, gets by in school, and is often overlooked both at home and in school.

4. *The Mascot.* This child distracts the family during times of heavy conflicts. The distractions may be in the form of entertainment or minor irritations. This child is usually a younger (or the youngest) sibling whom others try to protect from what is going on in the family. But he/she sees the fights and the drinking and knows that his/her antics can get other's attention. He/she is a nail biter who can't sit still. This child is immature, hyperactive, and boisterous in school and is the class clown.

5. *The Scapegoat.* This child "acts out" the family tension by developing a behavior pattern that serves as a camouflage to cover the parent's alcoholism. This child often is the second oldest and reacts to the positive attention the Family Hero gets by going in the other direction, defiantly trying to get attention by failing. He/she deflects attention from the alcoholic onto himself/herself. The worse the family situation gets, the worse this child behaves. This is the disruptive, substance-abusing child who's always in trouble in school."My friends are the only ones who understand me." "I didn't mean to get pregnant." "School's no fun; it's too hard." "We didn't really steal that car." Only the peer group matters, but they don't offer much. This child probably will drop out of school, if he/she isn't thrown out first. This person will have difficulty taking orders and keeping a job. If this child gets help early, there's a chance to turn him/her around.

Sometimes children combine roles as in Black's "Placater" role, which combines the behaviors of the Mascot and the Caretaker; occasionally, they will shift from one role to another, especially as older siblings leave home and vacate particular roles (66).

27

You never mess with Daddy when he comes home from work because he's "tired and under stress." If Daddy wants a beer, then you get up and get it for him, because you never want to upset him.

—Eileen, age 13

RULES

Wegscheider has described seven rules of unhealthy behavior patterns that are sustained in a chemically dependent family (67):

1. *The alcoholic's use of alcohol is the most important thing in the family's life.* Family members become as obsessed with the alcoholic's drinking as he/she is. Everything seems to revolve around this focal issue of family concern.
2. *Alcohol is not the cause of the family's problem.* Even when it's obvious, both the family and the alcoholic deny that the parent (or sibling, as the case may be) is an alcoholic.
3. *Someone or something else caused the alcoholic's dependency; he/she is not responsible.* The alcoholic and the family persist in blaming the problem on someone or something other than the alcoholic. Excuses may range from stress on the job to a bad marriage.
4. *The status quo must be maintained at all cost.* All family members strive to make it appear that everything's OK in the family, that nothing has changed.
5. *Everyone in the family must be an enabler.* Each family member enables the alcoholic to continue drinking by covering up, hiding, and accepting responsibility for the drinker.
6. *No one may discuss what really is going on in the family, either with one another or with outsiders.* This means that no open, honest communication takes place regarding the problem; and thus, the problem is never confronted nor is help sought or received.
7. *No one may say what he/she is really feeling.* Everyone in the family hides their feelings, keeps them to themselves, and eventually loses touch with how they honestly feel about the alcoholic, each other, and what is happening to them. This repression and denial of deep-seated feelings makes for unhappy and unfulfilled people.

Black has described the unwritten rules of the alcoholic family as "Don't Feel, Don't Talk, Don't Trust" (68).

Replacing these unhealthy "rules" and behaviors with healthy, honest, open ones is a goal of treatment for the alcoholic, the spouse, and the children.

RECOVERY

Living in a family with an alcoholic can be very stressful. But some families experience their greatest turmoil after the alcoholic or drug abuser is in treatment. This is because treatment requires all members of the family to become involved and forces them to think about and attempt to change the way they relate to one another.

> My Mom always made it a point to humiliate me in front of my friends. One time I was supposed to be home at 5:00 p.m. and I was like three minutes late and she started yelling at me in the middle of the driveway.
>
> —Brenda, age 12

Underlying family and personal problems do not necessarily go away once a person has stopped drinking or abusing drugs. For many children in families where drugs or alcohol are abused, even after the parent or sibling has begun treatment, life may continue to be very troubling (69).

In this book we speak of alcoholism/addiction as a disease. We believe it's important to see it that way because of how it affects our perception of the alcoholics/addicts and their children. Viewing alcoholism/addiction as a disease means that we can no more blame or stigmatize an alcoholic and his or her family than we can a victim of cancer or heart disease. This is important for us, just as it is important for the child of the alcoholic/addict, who must see himself/herself and the alcoholic in the family in a way that removes the sense of shame and blame. Parents who perceive drug and alcohol addiction as a disease also will be less prone to engage in denial of the problem because of guilt and shame They and the nonchemically dependent members of the family will be less apt to engage in behavior that enables the addict to continue abusing drugs/alcohol, and less likely to base their lives on the addict's condition.

There is little consensus on what constitutes effective therapy for alcoholism, or for that matter, drug addiction (70). Most treatment programs sooner or later direct their patients to join a support group such as AA or NA. Generally, people may become addicted to some drugs (like crack and heroin) more quickly than to alcohol. But the fundamental task of breaking the habit and starting over is the same. Recovery for both alcoholics and drug addicts is a lifelong struggle and relapses (or slips), particularly within the first year of abstinence, are not unusual.

Drug addiction treatment programs initially were modeled after alcohol treatment programs, but the influx of polydrug users has required many programs to change tactics, and the relapse rate of polydrug users tends to be even greater than it is among alcoholics (71). Today's substance abusers are more likely to abuse alcohol and other drugs simultaneously. Getting into treatment, of course, is only the beginning of a long procedure in recovery. As difficult as it is to abstain from using drugs or alcohol, it is even more difficult to remain abstinent. Recovery statistics, therefore, are poor. When all is said and done, the major burden for recovery lies with the substance abuser himself or herself.

> My Dad always had a beer in his hand and I just started taking sips. He thought it was cute. I don't like the taste of it, but I always wanted to drink it ... like my Dad.
>
> —Jim, age 16

Therefore, a family that has come to develop their relationships to one another around alcohol or drugs must make very big adjustments when one of its members goes into treatment. Children, and particularly grown children, may have to deal with long-suppressed anger about missing out on a normal childhood. The entire family may have to learn to live without a convenient scapegoat for every problem that comes along in the normal course of events. When the typical 28- or 30-day hospitalization, or residential-based initial recovery activity ends and the person in recovery returns home, the real struggle begins for all parties concerned (72). The substance abuser may then begin attending AA or NA and trying to work through his/her problems. Al-Anon and Alateen may help the spouse and children to focus on the issues that all must come to grips with and work out. This process may take years or even the rest of their lives.

When an addict or an alcoholic is recovering, the entire family is undergoing tremendous change and stress. The spouse of the abuser may unconsciously feel that the marriage is in jeopardy. A child may worry about becoming dispensable and that he/she is no longer able to play the traditional enabling role. Often the spouse or child may be made to feel guilty: "If you were a better wife/husband/son/daughter, maybe I wouldn't have started drinking." We know that the addict/alcoholic will always blame another person or situation for his/her problems. Recovery requires the individual to begin to face up to his/her own responsibility. But this is not easy, and the alcoholic/addict may continue to send the child mixed messages, just as he/she acted one way when sober or straight and very differently when drunk or high (73). This can be both confusing and frightening for children.

30

If the other adults in the alcoholic's life are confused about the behavior of the alcoholic and the delusion system in which he or she lives, imagine the child's difficulty in trying to make sense of the situation. Each family member has adapted to the chemically dependent person by developing behavior that causes the least amount of personal stress, no matter how unhealthy that behavior may be. For *family* recovery to begin, the following elements have to be present (74):

- *Recognition* of the alcohol/drug problem
- *Understanding* of the alcohol/drug problem (addictive disease)
- *Acceptance* of each family member's role in the problem.

And further along, each family member needs to understand that—

- He/she did not cause the other's drinking or drug taking
- He/she cannot solve the other person's problems
- He/she is a worthy and competent person in his/her own right.

As school employees, we cannot do anything about the other family members, but we can facilitate the recovery of the child.

THE TEACHER'S ROLE

As educators, we are not expected to diagnose the disease processes in the parents of our students, nor help get them into treatment. We need to know, however, that alcoholics are not able to control their drinking, that drinking causes problems in the lives of alcoholics, and that it can have devastating effects on the lives of their spouses and children. We need to know the nature of the disease process, that it can only get worse without intervention and treatment, and that even during the parent's or sibling's treatment, a child's stress and anxiety may persist.

It is important for the teacher and others who work with children to know the nature and symptoms of alcoholism and other addictions, but not to attempt to identify, label, or diagnose a family. Most often, the young child will not realize that the feelings he/she has, or that the discomfort and trauma within the family, are caused by alcoholism or drug addiction.

Students are affected differently by parental alcohol and drug abuse. Variables include birth order, role in the family, and the alcoholic's degree and type of addiction, as well as his/her response to the drugs or alcohol being used (75). The teacher's role is to know the basic facts about the disease, some factors common to families experiencing the illness, and the correct message to give to the students in his or her care. The classroom can be a safe haven, where students learn to overcome their handicaps, whether it be a learning disability, alcoholism in the family, or other factors that inhibit the learning process.

The environmental factors that may cause young people to abuse drugs have long been linked to a lackadaisical or permissive attitude toward drugs or alcohol in the family. Add to this the lack of structure, failure to develop appropriate coping or social skills, fears and anxieties, and poor self-image, and the likelihood of using and becoming addicted to alcohol or drugs for a child in such a family can be great indeed.

5. WHAT SCHOOLS CAN DO

About once a week we'd have to call the policeman who lived down
the street. The whole neighborhood knew, but we never talked about it
at home. I never talked about it to anyone before I came to group.

—Betsy, age 14

DRUG AND ALCOHOL EDUCATION

Because children of alcoholics/addicts are at high risk of becoming
drug and alcohol abusers themselves, they constitute a priority target
group for drug and alcohol prevention programs. Working with these
youngsters now may help alleviate their pain and may prevent them
from becoming substance abusers themselves. Effective prevention programs are well documented elsewhere, such as in the NEA's *How Schools
Can Help Combat Student Drug and Alcohol Abuse.* They include—

- learning about the effects of drugs and alcohol and the stages of experimentation, regular use, and dependency;
- developing and practicing techniques to resist pressure from peers
  and others to use drugs or alcohol;
- strengthening one's feeling of worth and competence;
- learning and practicing such social skills as decision making, problem solving, etc.

For children of alcoholics/addicts, drug and alcohol education must
also include discussions of the characteristics of parental drug and alcohol
abuse and its effects on the family. This brings it "out of the closet"
and communicates to the students that—

- it's an illness;
- it's not their fault;
- COAs run a greater risk than others of becoming addicted and
  must therefore be vigilant and careful;
- it can have serious effects on the family unless help is sought for
  those living with the alcoholic/addict;
- they are not alone; millions of other kids and families are going
  through the same experience;

33

- there is help available to them regardless of whether the alcoholic/ addicted parent seeks treatment.

There are a number of steps that schools can take to help meet the needs of children and youths whose parents are chemically dependent:

- We can learn more about drug addiction and alcoholism and their effects on the family; we can examine our own attitudes and experiences with alcohol and drugs, alcoholism and addiction, and alcoholics and addicts.
- We can teach our students about alcohol and drugs, and alcoholism and addiction, and their effects on families and children; we can lead older students to examine their own experiences and attitudes toward them.
- We can network with other community agencies to establish identification and referral procedures, provide support groups, and coordinate community efforts.
- We can help make parents aware of the nature and needs of children of alcoholics/addicts.
- We can help our students to improve their self-esteem by recognizing their strengths and abilities, and help to improve their ability to make good decisions and to exercise control in those areas of their lives that they're able to.
- We can set a good example, remembering that "little children have big ears" and that offhand comments about drinking to excess over the weekend or needing a valium for a headache can have a negative impact on students who overhear them.

IDENTIFYING CHILDREN OF ALCOHOLICS/ADDICTS

You don't need to know which of your students' parents abuse alcohol and drugs in order to provide them with effective drug and alcohol education. Simply provide the information, including the effects of alcoholism/addiction on families, to all students. The children of substance abusers will profit from this more than the others, but all students will benefit.

It is useful, however, to be able to identify the children of substance abusers so that additional attention and/or referral for other help can be provided. Ackerman lists the following student behaviors to look for during drug and alcohol education (77):

34

- Extreme negativism about alcohol and all drinking.
- Inability to think of healthy, integrative reasons and styles of drinking.
- Equation of drinking with getting drunk.
- Greater familiarity with different kinds of drinks than peers.
- Inordinate attention to alcohol in situations in which it is marginal, for example, in a play or movie not about drinking.
- Normally passive or distracted child becomes active or focused during alcohol discussions.
- Changes in attendance patterns during alcohol education activities.
- Frequent requests to leave the room.
- Lingering after activity to ask innocent question or simply to gather belongings.
- Mention of parent's drinking to excess on occasion.
- Mention of drinking problem of a friend's parent, uncle, or aunt.
- Strong negative feelings about alcoholics.

Other general indicators that may be helpful in identifying COAs in the school setting include (78)—

- Morning tardiness (especially Mondays).
- Consistent concern with getting home promptly at the end of a day or activity period.
- Malodorousness.
- Improper clothing for the weather.
- Regression: thumbsucking, bed-wetting, infantile behavior with peers.
- Scrupulous avoidance of arguments and conflict.
- Friendlessness and isolation.
- Poor attendance.
- Frequent illness and need to visit nurse, especially for stomach complaints.
- Fatigue and listlessness.
- Hyperactivity and inability to concentrate.
- Sudden temper tantrums and other emotional outbursts.
- Exaggerated concern with achievement and satisfying authority in children who are already at the head of the class, or similar behavior in social or athletic activities.

- Dramatic variations in academic performance from test to test and written assignment to written assignment.
- Extreme fear about situations involving contact with parents.
- Talk by other students about how things aren't so good at the COA's house.

Researchers are working to identify factors peculiar to children of alcoholics. Some studies have shown that more children of alcoholics perform poorly on some visual and memory tasks than do non-COAs. They believe that alcoholism is in part physical and genetic. Researchers believe that in the future we will have biological markers that will identify a vulnerability to drugs and alcohol in children (79). As the role of familial substance abuse in creating at-risk children attracts more attention, we can expect researchers who have hitherto focused exclusively on alcohol to focus on other drugs as well.

Although there are no foolproof criteria for identifying COAs, children's appearance, school performance, and peer group relationships provide clues to their identity (80). For example, children who come to school in soiled clothes and/or in a dirty, unkempt condition may be victims of an alcoholic parent's neglect. And youngsters with bruises or suspicious injuries may have been battered by a parent who becomes violent when drinking. Likewise, noticeable variations in performance or attendance may reflect a child's need to assume some of the alcoholic parent's responsibilities from time to time, such as housework and care of younger siblings, not to mention fear or anxiety following weekend binges and subsequent household violence.

Children of alcoholics/addicts may also be distinguished by keeping to themselves and resisting offers of friendship from peers. Or some may exhibit acting out or clownish behavior to attract attention. If such children do have friends, it may be only one; and they may be extremely demanding of that person's attention. School and/or community mental health professionals can administer tests developed to identify COAs, if there is sufficient cause for such referral.

In looking for signs of children and youth whose parents may be alcoholics/addicts, we need to recognize that specific behaviors or symptoms may have various explanations. Patterns of behavior, not single incidents or symptoms, are what we should look for; and even then we must be careful not to jump to conclusions or to label children (81).

Sometimes it's relatively easy to identify a child whose family life is overshadowed by alcoholism; for example, when the parent repeatedly turns up at school events drunk, or when a child confides in a teacher or counselor that his/her father comes home drunk every night and hits the mother. But these may not be frequent occurrences. Most of the time, school personnel do not see the parent under the influence of alcohol but can only observe the effects of the drinking such as the parent's absence from scheduled parent-teacher conferences, or the failure to sign and return report cards, or to respond to calls or notes from school (82).

An often-used method of identifying children of substance abusers is through drug and alcohol education. Class discussions that describe the progression of alcoholism and addiction and the characteristics of a drug or alcohol problem in the home can provide the teacher with an opportunity to elicit responses from students that may provide clues as to whether such a problem exists in a child's home. These opportunities can include invitations to see the counselor if any student knows someone who has a problem such as described and would like to learn how to get help (83). Sometimes students may use the opportunity offered by these discussions to give thinly veiled suggestions that they have this problem in their family. They may even contribute information to the class discussion that only people who are closely involved would know—for example, the time and location of Al-Anon meetings (84).

Sometimes parents or siblings may identify their family as needing help. At the end of community or parent meetings on drug/alcohol awareness, which include information on sources of help such as AA and Al-Anon, forms can be distributed, or left on the audience's chairs, asking people to indicate whether their children or those in a family that they know might be interested in participating in a support group.

After the principal introduced me and I began to show my slides and explain the Chapter I program of extra help in reading and math, one of the parents sprang out of her chair and began to rant, "What is this . . . ? My kid doesn't need any special program. She's doing fine." The principal tried to quiet her, but she jumped up several more times during my presentation before finally leaving the room, noisily jostling the chairs, her little girl in tow. I saw the little girl next day on the playground and said "Hi." She didn't make eye contact with me and didn't return my greeting.

—Elementary School Teacher

Likewise, an assembly or class meeting can be held on a health topic that includes the showing of films such as *Lots of Kids Like Us*, or *Feelings*, which target children and the problems they sometimes face in homes where drug or alcohol addiction exists. After seeing the films and

37

discussing how support groups work, children can be asked to complete a form indicating whether they or someone they know might be interested in—

- Signing up for a support group,
- Getting more information about it,
- Not pursuing it at this time.

Children Are People, a counseling and support organization geared to children of alcoholics, ages 5 to 12, recommends that a second form also be used, which youngsters bring home to parents, that includes information about the school's substance abuse prevention programs. A tear-off sheet at the bottom would include the same questions from a parent's viewpoint (85).

SUPPORT GROUPS

General information and discussion of alcoholism and drug addiction can be useful and beneficial for all students. But for children of substance abusers, more is required if they are to live in such an environment without serious short- and long-term harm befalling them. They need to know that—

- They are not unique;
- They are not at fault for what occurs in the family;
- They can develop trusting relationships with others that will not be violated;
- They are at particular risk for drug/alcohol abuse and must act accordingly.

These understandings as well as the opportunity to practice related social skills are best obtained in a support group such as Alateen or Al-Anon. Often, however, a smaller group may be more useful, especially if the child is younger and/or the family is in denial and does not acknowledge the problem or participate in a support group or in some kind of counseling. Support groups in schools, while not a substitute for longer-term, more intensive family intervention, do provide an opportunity for students living in alcoholic homes to (86)—

- Learn more about alcoholism/addiction as a family disease;
- Build self-esteem and increase self-awareness;

38

- Build trusting relationships with others, including an adult;
- Reduce their feeling of isolation and share feelings with others;
- Develop coping strategies for living in an alcoholic home.

Participating in a school group may help to prepare a child or adolescent for entering an Alateen group, which can be emotionally beneficial for teens (87). Such groups also provide an opportunity to deal with problems in school that may be directly or indirectly related to family substance abuse.

In secondary schools, participants may include children of substance abusers as well as non-COSAs who are recovering from drug/alcohol problems or who feel vulnerable and in need of support. Groups generally are led by school counselors and/or the school nurse, but sometimes a teacher may lead as well. Usually more than one adult leads the group, which may meet for only a limited number of weeks, or may be ongoing. Sometimes groups are run by individuals other than school staff, such as counselors from the local mental health agency or by a private group with whom the school system contracts. Prospective group members usually are first screened by the counselor who may also work with selected youngsters on an individual basis.

Prior to implementing support groups at the school, it is a good idea to make sure that people in charge, both in the school system and in the community, understand and back the need for such groups. Therefore, you will need to prepare—

1. A statement of needs
2. A description of how the support group will work
3. The goals and objectives of the group
4. The resources needed to implement the group.

Rather than presenting support groups for children of substance abusers as an isolated activity or program, it is a good idea to include them as part of the school's and community's overall response to the drug/alcohol problem. Consequently, strategies similar to those used in raising staff and community awareness of the student drug and alcohol problem can also be employed here. These may include sponsoring treatment workshops for staff and community members, and evening educational meetings where films are shown or speakers are sponsored. Key organizational representatives from the school system, mental health community, day-care centers, treatment centers, hospitals, social service agencies, and so on, should be invited to attend and participate as appropriate. The purpose of these events is to discuss how children are affected by drug and alcohol addiction in the family, the need they have for early intervention, and how they can be helped through support groups and other intervention activities.

Whether it's in a support group or through individual counseling, children in chemically dependent families need to work on (88)—

- Identifying and communicating feelings;
- Understanding that with regard to their parent's chemical dependence, they did not cause it, they cannot cure it, they can learn to cope with it;
- Recognizing their powerlessness over the alcoholic/addict in the family and over other people's emotions and behavior;
- Learning how alcoholism/addiction affects the entire family;
- Building a sense of trust with adults through their counselor, teacher, or group leader who function as consistent role models; and
- Practicing decision making, problem solving, goal-setting, and other social skills.

Usually support groups run anywhere from half an hour to one and one-half hours, although in school settings, most tend to be no more than 40 to 50 minutes in length, once a week. Often, the time of the support group meeting will rotate if it is during the school day so that children do not miss the same subject each week. Where feasible, however, groups can and do meet before or after school, thus obviating the need to pull a child out of class which, in addition to missing work, has the added disadvantage of creating a possible embarrassment for the child who may be asked by classmates where he or she is going. Most groups contain no more than eight or ten children so that each child has an opportunity to participate fully. Rules of respect and order are closely followed. Some community support groups are held in the early evening or in late afternoon after school, depending on transportation, baby sitting, etc. If a school schedule is such that there is an activity period or a convenient time during the school day to meet, this can be utilized instead. Groups can meet in schools, at community centers, or other appropriate places where it is comfortable, clean, and safe.

The right to confidentiality in a support group is essential, whether it's AA, Al-Anon, Alateen, or a group set up for younger children of alcoholics. Children may choose to discuss the group with their parents or others, but they need to know that they do not have to. They also need to know that no one else will divulge what goes on in the meeting, nor are they to discuss what anyone else said or did in the group.

It is important, however, to tell children right from the start about child protection laws, which in most states require that even a suspicion of physical and sexual abuse of a child must be reported by adult care-givers. It is important, therefore, to explain when discussing the rule on "what is said in group stays in group," that people who work with children have to report it if they think the child is being harmed or abused. The group leader should describe in simple, understandable terms what is meant by physical and sexual abuse. The leader should also invite children in the group to tell her/him in private if any of those things are happening to them so that the leader can tell someone and try to get help for them. Before dealing with this issue, group leaders should thoroughly acquaint themselves with their school district's policies and with their state's laws on this subject.

> He could do anything from be really nice to really mean when he was high. Sometimes he beat on my Mom and when she wasn't around, he'd beat on me.
>
> —John, age 16

Children Are People, which runs groups for youngsters 5 to 12 years of age and provides training to others so that they can run their own groups, mixes children of all ages and their siblings in a large group and then breaks them up by age and family during small-group segments. They report that having siblings in the same small group helps to break down the "no talking" family rule described by Claudia Black (89). This is the unwritten rule in drug/alcohol-addicted families that says family members do not discuss the drinking or drug use or their feelings about it with each other or with others outside the family. Many school-based groups are organized according to age and grade level, with a span of no more than two or three years or grades. Thus, K-3 students might be in one group and fourth through sixth graders in another. This also makes it easier to gear lesson plans for topic presentations since children are in the same general developmental range.

PARENTAL INVOLVEMENT

The basic assumption is that almost all parents care about their children and want the best for them; therefore, some parents will send their children to group even if they themselves are not dealing with their own problems. Sometimes social service agencies or the courts will refer children to groups (90).

41

Sometimes, either in conjunction with, or as a follow-up to a support group activity, parents will be invited to participate in "parenting" or "communication" workshops. Although neither the addicted nor the nonaddicted parent will often participate, it still is worth pursuing their participation. Before involving the child in a support group or counseling activity, the parents should be notified for a number of reasons:

- Because of the sensitive nature of what may be discussed in group and in counseling with COAs, administrators, teachers, and counselors will all feel better if they cannot be accused of going behind the parents' backs and invading the family's privacy.
- A parent may be needed to bring the child to and from the group, depending on when it meets.
- It provides an opportunity to encourage parents to seek help for their children and to make referrals for them to other agencies.

STAFF AWARENESS

Another way in which to help children of substance abusers is for school personnel to become aware of the process and characterisitics of chemical dependence and how parental alcoholism/addiction affects children. The number of students in our schools who live with parental alcoholism/addiction is a large one, yet few school staff members understand this family disease. Therefore, their ability to assist these students effectively, or even to understand them, is limited.

All school staff—teachers, aides, administrators, and counselors—should raise their level of awareness. One way to accomplish this is by attending workshops on this topic. As a practical matter, in order to reach all staff, such a workshop would need to be offered after school or on a workday or half-day set aside for staff development activities. A "Workshop Leader's Guide," by Rita Rumbaugh, is provided in Chapter 6 to assist school staff in conducting such a workshop.

Another suggestion for raising one's awareness of this problem is to attend an AA or Al-Anon meeting. Attendance at an Alcoholics Anonymous meeting can help one appreciate the fact that alcoholics are ill, not bad or immoral, and that their children are not to be avoided, tolerated, stereotyped, or even "protected." Teachers, like others, have grown up with a variety of myths about alcoholism that may make them reluctant to acknowledge the disease, let alone confront it either in their students' families or in their own. Very few of us do not have a relative, friend, or acquaintance unaffected by alcoholism/addiction. Dealing with one's own feelings and beliefs about alcoholism/addiction can be an important component of a staff workshop and/or a visit to an AA meeting. Each of us can learn a great deal about alcoholism/addiction land the process of recovery by attending an AA meeting. Most cities and towns in the United States have many AA meetings at all times of the day and night, each day of the week. Some are designated as "open" and others as "closed."

Open meetings are ones that anyone who is interested in the AA program may attend. At open meetings, speakers who are recovering alcoholics tell their personal stories of what their life was like when they were practicing alcoholics, and how they are recovering through the AA program. Closed meetings are for alcoholics only; the purpose is to discuss the AA 12-Step program of recovery and to give individual members the opportunity to ask questions and express themselves freely (91). In addition to AA and Al-Anon, Alateen, Narcotics Anonymous, Adult Children of Alcoholics, and Tough Love, to name a few, are other support organizations that probably have chapters in your locale. A perusal of the telephone book should give you a number to call locally for more information; or you can contact the national headquarters of these organizations listed in the Appendix. Many metropolitan areas publish separate "Where and When Directories," available for a nominal fee, listing the locations and times of AA and Al-Anon/Alateen meetings, as well as whether the meetings are open or closed.

COUNSELING, INTERVENTION, REFERRAL

It's important to remind ourselves that school staff seldom are trained as alcohol or addiction counselors. Teachers' roles, as with any other troubled child, should be to be aware of and alert to symptoms and signs of a problem. Teachers should be both willing and able to be supportive and sensitive to a child's needs as well as knowledgeable about where and how to refer children for help.

Counselors and other pupil services professionals, of course, may go further. They should show children of substance abusers who are referred to them that they understand how the students feel and may counsel them on a preliminary basis. Morehouse and Scola suggest that once the student has described the family situation and his or her concerns, the next step is for the counselor (or teacher) to educate the child about alcoholism/addiction (92). This first step is important in helping the child feel less disturbed about the drinking. It is also helpful in correcting distorted perceptions about the parent's behavior that a young child may find bewildering and frightening. Ultimately, the child will need to

43

be referred to a support group or community agency for help. This, of course, must be done through the parent, except when the counselor suspects abuse or mistreatment of the child by the parent.

The important thing to remember is that schools generally are not in the treatment business. This is best left to other agencies. The school may perform initial counseling, intervention, and referral. It may cooperate with outside agencies in conducting support group activities on the premises. Sometimes it may even conduct support groups on its own. More commonly, however, schools will provide drug and alcohol education, education that includes helping at-risk children develop skills to cope with their problems.

Admittedly, the line between education and treatment may sometimes be blurred. Certainly, in the eyes of the law it is a fuzzy, ill-defined separation (93). Some professionals believe that if they have to wait for acknowledgment of parental alcoholism/addiction or parents' permission to participate in a program, children of alcoholics/addicts, especially younger children, will rarely receive the help they need.

> God grant me the serenity
> to accept the things I cannot change,
> the courage to change the things I can,
> and the wisdom
> to know the difference
> —Reinhold Niebuhr

Nevertheless, legal and ethical considerations dictate that schools must inform parents of any special help or counseling their children are receiving. Since most parents want what is best for their children, this rarely presents a problem, especially if the school is tactful in its communication with the home. If permission is denied and the home situation appears to be one that jeopardizes the child's health, safety, and welfare, child protection and juvenile court authorities should be alerted.

Brake advises counselors to help children realize that they can love their parents without liking what they do (94). She believes group counseling can help COAs to feel better about themselves as valued and worthwhile individuals and to understand that they can attend to many of their own needs for happiness, regardless of how their parents behave. Counselors can establish themselves as dependable, trustworthy adults in the COAs' eyes by being on time for meetings, keeping their word, and asking the child's permission before discussing his or her situation with anyone else (95).

Burwick and others list three strategies for intervention with children whose parents are chemically dependent (96). Although they are directed at school counselors, they may well apply to teachers and other school personnel who come into regular contact with these children.

1. *Model consistency.* A stable environment with set roles and boundaries is just what is missing in the COAs' home life. A classroom and school day that is not confusing and does not abruptly change is needed, as are adults who are neither too permissive nor too authoritarian.

2. *Respond to both adaptive and maladaptive behavior.* Such children are in extreme need of positive feedback and recognition for positive, constructive behaviors. Similarly, COAs also need to have appropriate and immediate consequences for negative behavior. This shows the child that you care.

3. *Enable children to succeed.* Do not be overprotective of children of alcoholics/addicts; but do look for uninvolved or withdrawn children who may need help in how to interact with peers.

Morehouse and Scola speak of the reluctance of many school personnel to approach known children of alcoholics/addicts, because they "feel they are accusing a student of something when it comes to parental alcoholism [and addiction]" (97). If this applies to you, it may be that deep inside you still feel that there is something evil about people who are chemically dependent and that that evil rubs off on the child. Think about it. If the student's parent had cancer or was dying from some other disease, you wouldn't hesitate to express sincere and friendly concern about the stress the illness must be causing the student and the family to suffer. You'd also offer to put the student in touch with someone to talk to who might help him/her to better deal with the stress. Why not treat the child of an alcoholic or addicted parent in the same way?

The person to whom teachers should make referrals typically will be the counselor or pupil services specialist in their school or district. This person should have a detailed knowledge of resources in the community. Such resources include Al-Anon, Alateen, Adult Children of Alcoholics, and other support groups and organizations. Additionally, local hospitals, clinics, and private physicians, churches and synagogues, social service agencies, health departments, and other government services such as shelters, crisis hot lines, and family counseling programs are valuable resources to be familiar with.

When assessing the programming needs of children brought to the attention of administrators, pupil services specialists, and special educators, the possibility of parental and/or sibling chemical dependence should be considered. Appropriate intervention may mean an alternative program or a special placement but it might also mean group support and counseling for issues stemming from parental alcoholism/addiction. Youngsters presenting characteristics such as chronic truancy, disruptive behavior, substance abuse, promiscuity/pregnancy, and poor grades may be candidates for Alateen. Parental addiction must be included on any checklist of at-risk behavior causes and needs. Too often, it is not considered.

STUDENT ASSISTANCE PROGRAMS

Because parental substance abuse puts children at such high risk for drug and alcohol abuse, many schools regard this problem as an aspect of the overall student drug and alcohol abuse problem. A popular system that incorporates a comprehensive approach to the problem of helping students deal with all the ways they're affected by their own or someone else's substance abuse is the Student Assistance Program model. This model typically performs six basic functions in the school (98):

1. Early identification of actual or potential substance abusers;
2. Assessment, or gathering of data about the suspected student to determine the type and extent of abuse;
3. Intervention in the problem, referral to individuals or agencies that are equipped to provide treatment and support to the student in the form of groups and/or individual counseling;
4. Clarification of roles and structures so that staff, students, and parents all know and agree on who will perform each of the functions required;
5. Support from appropriate policy and operating procedures that spell out expected behavior and consequences;
6. Staff training regarding drugs and related issues.

Student Assistance Programs (SAP) often represent a collaborative effort between the school and the local mental health agency that supplies trained addiction counselors to work in the school several days a week and implement the SAP with school staff. This is known as the "externally based" SAP model. Sometimes in a "core team" model, a group of school-based staff, usually including an administrator, a counselor, a nurse, and perhaps a teacher or aide, will work together to coordinate the model after each has received specialized training. A third model is

46

the "internally based" program, in which the school hires its own specially trained addiction counselors to implement the program. Each model has its assets and liabilities, but generally the value of the SAP model is in its comprehensive approach to drug and alcohol abuse (99).

CLASSROOM ACTIVITIES

As a classroom teacher, there are a number of steps you can take to help children whose parents are chemically dependent. A knowledge of, and sensitivity to chemical dependence and its effects on the family are important. When children are small, they have not yet learned to "keep the secret" and are more apt to tell the teacher about what goes on at home. The younger they are when they get help, the better will be their chance of coping as they get older. Teachers who have students who attend a support group or receive counseling during the school day should allow the student out of class, and try to help the student make up work and not feel out of place. Classroom teachers also can assist students by helping them to feel valued, wanted, and competent; by encouraging them to make and sustain friendships; and by helping them to realize that they are not alone and that help is available. These children do not need our sympathy, they need our understanding and skill.

If we suspect that youngsters are abusing drugs or alcohol, our obligation and course is clear: express concern, offer help, consult with colleagues, notify parents, and refer them for help. Older children are seriously at risk of slipping into chemical abuse and we should be alert to this danger. Just as with student substance abuse, if we see any indications of parental addiction, for example, in student writing assignments, we must never ignore them. Referral to a pupil services specialist is essential. The risk of violent abuse also is something we should be vigilant for. Know your obligations for reporting problems and be aware of tell-tale signs (100). Remain alert to the needs and behaviors of your students. Your accurate observations of students can be helpful to specialists and colleagues and to professionals outside the school when referring children for help.

In general, teachers should (101)—

- Try not to be overprotective or solicitous; be matter of fact, friendly, and responsible.
- Increase their knowledge of alcoholism/addiction so they can answer questions such as, "What is alcohol/drugs?" "Why do people drink/take drugs?" "Do you drink/take drugs?" Be prepared to give clear factual information, if asked.

47

- Create a class environment that is psychologically and emotionally safe. This means that your behavior should be predictable, consistent, and fair.
- Facilitate the development of peer relationships and activities that decrease isolation and increase the child's social skills and sense of identity, apart from the parental alcoholism/addiction.

The United States Office of Substance Abuse Prevention also suggests that teachers and other caregivers (102)—

- Maintain a small library of books and pamphlets on alcohol and drug-related topics that have been written for children (see Appendix A).
- Be sensitive to cultural differences and have colleagues with whom you can consult on such issues.
- Be aware that children of alcoholics/addicts may be threatened by displays of affection, especially physical contact.
- Always follow through if a child of an alcoholic/addict asks you for help.
- Make sure the child understands three basic facts: (1) He/she is not alone; there are millions of children of alcoholics under age 20 in the United States. (2) He/she is not responsible for the problem and cannot control the parent's drinking (or drug-taking) behavior. (3) He/she is a valuable, worthwhile individual.
- Don't act embarrassed or uncomfortable when a child asks you for help. It may be discouraging for the child and increase his or her sense of isolation and hopelessness.
- Don't criticize the child's parents or be overly sympathetic.
- Do not share the child's problems with others who do not have a need to know.
- Don't make plans with the child if you can't keep the date. Stability and consistency in relationships are necessary in order for the child to develop trust.
- Don't try to help the child by yourself unless you are trained to do so. Refer the child to appropriate helping professionals and assist as requested.

Teachers also should be watchful for developmental problems. For example, when children are seven- or eight-years-old, they are just getting past "magical" thinking, regarding their parents as all powerful, beginning to see them in perspective to others around them. With an alcoho-

48

lic/addict in the family, this myth is shattered. At a stage of development where fairness is important, children can become outraged over the lack of fairness that may exist in their family. Each stage of a child's development has tasks to be completed, if the child is to develop normally. Children of substance abusers often have those tasks interfered with, and must try in later life, when it is much more difficult, to accomplish them (e.g., developing autonomy). One of those tasks is learning to socialize (103). We can help youngsters learn to socialize by pairing withdrawn children with peers who have good socialization skills.

Because a positive self-image depends heavily on self-acceptance, teachers who wish to help students develop a positive self-image should help them to (104)—

- Feel good about themselves by giving them positive messages and by showing them how to give themselves positive messages, telling kids what they do right;
- Work to their potential by expressing appropriate expectations for them and by giving them tasks they can accomplish that are neither too easy nor too difficult;
- Exercise self-discipline, keep themselves in control, and not allow others to trigger negative behavior in them;
- Develop a strong sense of purpose such as doing well in school, sports, and hobbies, and making and maintaining friendships;
- Take responsibility for their own actions and learn from their own mistakes; and
- Develop a sense of humor so that they can joke about themselves and see that it's OK to make mistakes.

These are insights and skills that all children need, but children of alcoholics/addicts are in critical need of them. Teachers have a significant effect on children and how they develop. This help at school in developing healthy outlooks and needed social skills may be what at-risk children require in order to see themselves as individuals apart from family addictions and thus prevent subsequent personal tragedy and failure, and achieve self-realization.

6. WORKSHOP LEADER'S GUIDE

by Rita Rumbaugh

To make maximum use of the foregoing information, a workshop based on this manual may be offered to school staff. This workshop, "Children of Alcoholics in School," is designed to be presented to school staff in three working sessions of 45-60 minutes each, or in one staff in-service of three hours. Only basic information will be presented as an introduction to the topic; much of the material used is based on information provided in previous chapters of this book. If a shorter period of time is required, some activities or films can be deleted. Additional resources and activities are listed at the end of the guide for further learning in an expanded time frame.

CAUTION

Please be aware of possible denial and resistance of staff who may be adult children of alcoholics, spouses of alcoholics, or active alcoholics. The workshop and the material presented will be uncomfortable and troubling to them. You may meet with a great deal of criticism. Be prepared for it. Have confidence in your material. You may wish to preface your workshop by bringing in a speaker from Adult Children of Alcoholics or Al-Anon to help create a receptive audience.

WORKSHOP SESSION 1

GOAL

To introduce the staff to the feelings, needs, and characteristics of students who are in families where the use of alcohol and/or other drugs cause problems.

OBJECTIVES

The staff will—

1. List the characteristics of the alcoholic parent, spouse, and child.
2. Describe codependency and enabling (see pp. 25–26).
3. Identify family roles (pp. 26–28).

50

Materials and Resources Needed

Newsprint, markers
Film, *Soft Is the Heart of a Child*
Tape newsprint in pattern: *1   2/4   3*
Speaker from Al-Anon or Adult Children of Alcoholics

INTRODUCTION

1. Create an informal atmosphere to discuss the "feeling disease" of alcoholism. Arrange the room by structuring seating in horseshoe pattern (no tables or desks in front of participants).
2. Preface the workshop with the recollections of a speaker from Adult Children of Alcoholics or Al-Anon. Ask the speaker to talk about what it's like to grow up in an alcoholic or dysfunctional household.
3. Use materials in this book, pages 7–10, to create awareness of statistics and extent of problem of alcohol use and dependency.

ACTIVITY

1. Arrange four sheets of newsprint on the wall as described above.
2. Ask staff to brainstorm the characteristics of the addict in the family. Determine whether the addict is he (father) or she (mother). Validate each response; do not evaluate or clarify until the brainstorming is ended. List the characteristics as the staff identify them on the far right paper (3). Ask staff to clarify the characteristics that need further explanation. Validate and encourage staff response.
3. On far left paper (1), ask staff to brainstorm the characteristics of the spouse (male or female) of the addict. List and clarify as before. Briefly explain the codependency of the spouse.
4. On the middle sheet (2), write son/daughter. Stand in the middle between the two sheets (1) and (3), list the characteristics of the addict and the spouse and ask, "What does it feel like to be a child in this family?" List and clarify the feelings of the child/children.
5. Ask how these feelings may be translated into students' behavior and list on sheet (4).
6. Emphasize the nature of the family disease and the "don't talk" and "don't trust," "don't feel" rules. Explain "the conspiracy of silence" and "codependency."

51

7. Categorize the behavior traits of the child listed on sheet 4 into "roles" and describe each role briefly.
8. Show film, *Soft Is the Heart of a Child*. The film is somewhat dated, but clearly portrays the family dilemma.

PROCESSING ACTIVITY

1. List the family role portrayed by each child in the movie.
2. What were the feelings of each child? The feelings of the mother?
3. Imagine you were a teacher in the school serving these students. What would your feelings be about each of these children?

CLOSURE

Ask staff to be aware of any children that might fit the role descriptions listed for the next workshop session.

WORKSHOP SESSION 2

GOAL

To explore family disease and family roles in an addictive family.

OBJECTIVES

The staff will—

1. Define family disease progression and dynamics (pp. 23–25).
2. Identify family roles and family rules (pp. 26–28).
3. Describe why children of alcoholics should be identified and helped (pp. 18–22)

Materials and Resources Needed

Newsprint, markers, "Stamp Game"
Film, *Lots of Kids Like Us*
Handouts from Adult Children of Alcoholics, Al-Anon, Children of Alcoholics (see Appendix B)
Posters from Al-Anon, Alateen, and the National Children of Alcoholics Association

INTRODUCTION

1. Introduce the "Stamp Game" to staff, asking for volunteers to play. Explain that the game is useful with children who do not "feel, trust, or talk." (See Appendix A, p. 66.)
2. Ask volunteers to use the feeling cards to describe their thoughts and feelings about the topic—"Children of Alcoholics in School."
3. Look for, encourage, and support staff members who are adult children of alcoholics to self-disclose to the rest of the group.

ACTIVITY

1. Present the "Family Disease" progression and dynamics by listing the four stages of the disease. Explain the delusion and denial of the addict and the enabling system in the family, as described on pages 25–26.
2. Ask staff to divide into three groups: eldest, middle, and youngest children. Subdivide the groups, if they are too large.
3. Designate an area of the room for each group to work.
4. The groups' task is to describe and list the feelings and behavior of being the eldest, middle, or youngest child. Then ask them to use the designated terms as mascot, hero, and lost child. Explain that all families have these roles to some degree. A dysfunctional or alcoholic family's roles are rigid and confining to the family members and have an impact on the child in school.
5. Explain that we have already begun the next generation of addicts. Use the statistics regarding risk factors on pages 7–8 to alert staff to the necessity of prevention with children of alcoholics.
6. Show film, *Lots of Kids Like Us*.

PROCESSING QUESTION

How do the statistics cited compare to what you perceive as the problem at this school?

CLOSURE

Usually some vulnerable or affected staff members will have disclosed their family history by this time. It will be necessary to support them while setting the stage for the next workshop session. Remind staff of time and date of Session 3.

WORKSHOP SESSION 3

GOAL

To identify children who may be in alcoholic families and design an action plan to help them in the school setting.

OBJECTIVES

The staff will—

1. Describe behaviors of children who may be at risk as low-achieving, behavior problems, truant, and abused.
2. Describe programs that address the needs of these students. Discuss specific mechanisms within the school to help identify children in alcoholic families. Formulate action plans to help these children.
3. Practice messages that may be given to children regarding dysfunctional or alcoholic families (e.g., "You didn't cause it," "You can't cure it," "You can learn to cope with it," and "There are millions of others just like you").

Materials and Resources Needed

Video, *Tell Someone*
Newsprint, markers, "Stamp Game"
NCOA Newsletter, "Kids Like Us"
Do's and Don'ts (National Clearinghouse for Alcohol Information)
Messages printed on cards or xeroxed for handout
Children Are People curriculum manual
ACOAs' Where and When Directory of meetings in your area
Al-Anon Where and When Directory of meetings in your area

INTRODUCTION

1. Arrange seating as before. Display Al-Anon and ACOA posters and message signs.
2. Introduce "Stamp Game" again and ask for volunteers. Ask volunteers to use the feeling cards to describe a situation in which they were concerned about a particular child who may come from an alcoholic home.

ACTIVITY

1. Brainstorm the characteristics of children who may be at risk and list on newsprint. Brainstorm the characteristics of children of alcoholics in the same school setting. Compare and contrast the lists.

2. Describe programs within the school for children at risk. Ask if these programs would reach the children of alcoholics. Why? Why not? How could these programs be adjusted to reach these children?

3. Ask "What other mechanisms currently exist to identify children of alcoholics in the school setting?" Encourage staff to find mechanisms within the school setting to identify these children.

4. Show video, *Tell Someone*.

5. Post the messages all staff can give to all students in either an alcoholic or any dysfunctional family. Explain the role that all staff have in helping children of alcoholics (pp. 33–49).

The 4 Cs message to children of alcoholics:

"C – Cause"	You didn't *cause* it. It's not your fault that mom or dad is chemically dependent.
"C – Cure"	Alcoholism is a disease and you can't *cure* it.
"C – Control"	You can't *control* mom's or dad's drinking or drug use. You can only control your response to it.
"C – Cope"	You can *cope*! You can learn coping strategies and seek out people who can help you cope.

6. If an elementary school, show the Children Are People support group manual for staff review and comments. Explain the program briefly.

   If a secondary school, explain Alateen support groups for students. Display Alateen posters and distribute Al-Anon/Alateen Where and When Directory to participants.

7. Designate one staff contact person for questions/concerns regarding children of alcoholics and further training.

ADDITIONAL RESOURCES AND ACTIVITIES

The following videotapes are excellent for staff training in an expanded time frame.

Workshop Session 1

Child's View, with Claudia Black, uses pictures and stories written by children to explain alcoholism.

Workshop Session 2

Roles, with Claudia Black, and the *Family Trap*, with Sharon Wegscheider-Cruse, depict the rigidity of role definition in alcoholic families.

Workshop Session 3

Alateen videotape, *Alateen Tells It Like It Is*, as told by children from alcoholic families, shows the teens' viewpoint.

Follow the video with a discussion and process questions.

APPENDIXES

A. RESOURCES

For Staff

Films, Videos

Children of Alcoholics. 38 min. 1982. Designed for use with therapists, counselors, and other professionals, this videocassette features Dr. Robert Ackerman discussing the special treatment needs in working with children of alcoholics and their families. Available from Addiction Research and Consulting Services, 116 Cambridge Street, Indiana, PA 15701.

Children of Alcoholics. 30 min. 1981. Sharon Wegscheider explores the development of dysfunctional behavior patterns that become normal survival techniques for children of alcoholics. In understanding these roles, we are better equipped to help children choose to change. Provides understanding, compassion, and support. Available from Onsite Training and Consulting, Inc., 2820 W. Main Street, Rapid City, SD 57702.

Children of Denial. 28 min., color. Alcoholism Children Therapy (ACT), P.O. Box 8536, Newport Beach, CA 92660.

Children of Denial. 28 min. VHS. Dr. Claudia Black, therapist, discusses the denial often present in COAs and how they learn not to talk, not to trust, and not to feel. For professionals and interested adults.

A Child's View. 36 min. 1987. Dr. Claudia Black uses pictures to explain to children about alcohol and drug abuse. Available from M.A.C., 1850 High Street, Denver, CO 80218.

Everyone a Winner. 4 min. 1981. Breakfast-time conflict in a family is resolved with anger, door-slamming, and retreat. Alone, the wife turns to two comforts—a drink and a phone call to mother. A short open-ended film intended to trigger discussion. Available from National Publications, P.O. Box 4116, Omaha, NE 68104.

A Family Talks About Alcohol. 30 min. 1983. Dramatizes the problems experienced by a family with one alcoholic member. Junior and senior high. Available from Perennial Education, Inc., 930 Pitner Avenue, Evanston, IL 60202.

Francesca Baby. 45 min. 1981. Two daughters, ages 16 and 10, attempt to cope with their mother's alcoholism. Portrays the effects on the daughters and the beginnings of recovery through Alateen. Appropriate for adolescent and adult audiences. Available from Walt Disney Studios, Burbank, CA 91505.

Hope for the Children. 28 min. 1984. Problems faced by 5- to 12-year-old children of alcoholics as well as vignettes from therapy groups. Designed to train and motivate adults to intervene. Available from Health Communications, Inc., 1721 Blount Road, Suite 1, Pompano Beach, FL 33069.

Hope for the Children: Early Intervention with Kids from Alcoholic Homes. 30 min., color. Available for free loan courtesy of Operation Cork, Modern Talking Picture Service, Inc., 5000 Park Street North, St. Petersburg, FL 33709.

Lots of Kids Like Us. 28 min. 1983. A small boy and his sister try to cope with their father's alcoholism. Gives children the messages: "You are not alone," and "It's not your fault." Available from Gerald T. Rogers Productions, Inc., 5225 Old Orchard Road, Suite 23, Skokie, IL 60077. (312) 967-8080.

Roles. 42 min. 1987. Four roles of children of alcoholics called the "Responsible One," the "Adjuster," the "Placater," and the "Acting-Out One" are presented and discussed by Dr. Claudia Black. Available from M.A.C., 1850 High Street, Denver, CO 80218.

She Drinks a Little. 31 min. 1981. Teenager Cindy Stott has an alcoholic mother whose drinking is destroying both their lives. With the help of a male classmate with a similar problem, Cindy discovers Alateen and learns how to deal with her mother. Available from Learning Corporation of America, 1350 Avenue of the Americas, New York, NY 10019.

Soft Is the Heart of a Child. 30 min. 1980. Depicts the effects of alcoholism on the family. The focus is on the trauma of the children and the need for professionals to respond. This film is particularly effective with school personnel and concerned adults. Available from Gerald T. Rogers Productions, 5225 Old Orchard Road, Suite 23, Skokie, IL 60077. (312) 967-8080.

A Story About Feelings. 10 min. 1981. Uses cartoons to teach 5- to 8-year-old children how drinking, using drugs, and smoking are unwise choices for changing one's feelings. Family services, children's organizations, and prevention agencies can use this film to help children understand and express their feelings. Available from Hazelden Press, Pleasant Valley Road, Center City, MN 55012-0176.

Substance Abuse: Fetal Alcohol Syndrome. Part I, 57 min. 1983. Includes a presentation by expert scientists, panel discussions and questions from a coast-to-coast audience. Topics include alcohol, tobacco, and caffeine. Available from National Center for Education in Maternal and Child Health, 38th and R Streets, NW, Washington, DC 20057.

The Summer We Moved to Elm Street. 30 min. 1968. The family of an alcohol ic is shown through the eyes of a 9-year-old daughter. Available from McGraw-Hill Films, 330 W. 42nd Street, New York, NY 10036.

That's Marilyn. 28 min. 1980. This dramatic program about the children of alcoholics provides an understanding of some of the sufferings of thousands of young people in our communities. Designed for teenage and adult audiences, this video will spark a sympathetic discussion on these issues. Available from Aims Media, Inc., 626 Hustin Avenue, Glendale, CA 91201.

Printed Matter

Ackerman, R. J. *Children of Alcoholics: Bibliography and Resource Guide*. 3d ed. Pompano Beach, FL: Health Communications, 1987.

_____. *Children of Alcoholics: A Guidebook for Educators, Therapists, and Parents*. Holmes Beach, FL: Learning Publications, 1978. Outlines developmental phases and personality formation of children of alcoholics and the roles of schools, teachers, administrators, and therapists in working with them.

_____. *Let Go and Grow: Recovery for Adult Children*. Pompano Beach, FL: Health Communictions, 1987.

_____, ed. *Growing in the Shadow*. Pompano Beach, FL: Health Communications, 1986.

Al-Anon Family Group. *One Day at a Time in Alateen*. New York: Al-Anon Family Group Headquarters, 1984.

Anderson E. E., and Quast, W. "Young Children in Alcoholic Families: A Mental Health Needs-Assessment, and an Intervention Prevention Strategy." *Journal of Primary Prevention* 3 (1983): 174-87.

Benedict, Elizabeth. *The Beginner's Book of Dreams*. New York: Alfred A. Knopf, 1988.

Bepko, Claudia. *The Responsibility Trap: A Blueprint for Treating the Alcoholic Family*. New York: Free Press, 1985.

Black, C. "Children of Alcoholics." *Alcohol Health and Research World* 41, no. 1 (1979): 23-27.

_____. "The Family Law in Alcoholic Homes—Don't Talk." In *Changing Legacies*, edited by Health Communications, 39-42. Hollywood, FL: Health Communications, 1984.

_____. "Innocent Bystanders at Risk; The Children of Alcoholics." *Alcoholism* 1, no. 3 (1981): 22-26.

_____. *It Will Never Happen to Me.* Denver: Medical Administration Co., Printing and Publications Division, 1982. Presents survival techniques used by youngsters living with an alcoholic and problems childhood behavior can cause in adulthood. Includes information on therapy for adult children of alcoholics, family violence, and resources for help.

_____. *Repeat After Me.* Denver: Medical Administration Co., 1985.

_____. "Conflict and Crisis Typify Life for Children from Alcoholic Families." In *Changing Legacies*, edited by Health Communications, 37-38. Hollywood, FL: Health Communications, 1984.

Bornmaster, J., and Treat, C. *Building Interpersonal Relationships through Talking, Listening, Communicating: Group Activities for Students of All Ages.* Austin, TX: PRO-ED, 1982.

Brennan, Gale P. *I Know They Love Me Anyway.* Milwaukee: DePaul Rehabilitation Hospital, 1986.

Brenner, Avis. *Helping Children Cope with Stress.* Lexington, MA: Lexington Books, 1984.

Brisbane, Francis Larry. "A Report from the National Black Alcoholism Council on Black Children of Alcoholic and Drug Addicted Parents." Chicago: National Black Alcoholism Council, 1987.

Brown, Stephanie. *Treating Adult Children of Alcoholics, A Developmental Perspective.* New York: John Wiley & Sons, 1988.

Burnett, Carol. *One More Time.* New York: Random House, 1986.

Califano, Joseph A., Jr. *Report on Drug Abuse and Alcoholism.* New York: Warner Books, 1982. What everyone should know about addiction and ways individuals, industry, and government can help to combat it.

Chandler, Mitzi. *Whiskey's Song.* Pompano Beach, FL: Health Communications, 1987.

Children of Alcoholics Foundation. *Directory of National Resources for Children of Alcoholics.* New York: COA Foundation, 1986. A comprehensive state-by-state listing and description of programs that provide direct and indirect services and support to children of alcoholics. A very useful reference work that includes addresses, telephone numbers, description of services, admission criteria, fees, financial assistance . . . and more.

_____. *Report of the Conference on Research Needs and Opportunities for Children of Alcoholics.* New York: COA Foundation, 1985. The Research Conference sponsored by the Children of Alcoholics Foundation in April 1984, brought together 18 leaders in clinical medicine and research to review current knowledge about the effects of alcoholism on the family, identify priority research needs and opportunities, and recommend strategies for encouraging such research. Available from Children of Alcoholics Foundation (free).

Coltoff, Philip, and Luks, Allan. *Prevent Child Maltreatment: Begin with the Parent*. New York: Children's Aid Society, 1978.

Cork, R. M. *The Forgotten Children*. Toronto: Alcohol and Drug Addiction Research Foundation, 1969. A straightforward report of a study of 125 children of alcoholics that describes their feelings about themselves and their parents.

Dean, Amy E. *Once Upon a Time: Stories from Adult Children*. Center City, MN: Hazelden Foundation, 1987.

Deutsch, Charles. *Broken Bottles, Broken Dreams: Understanding and Helping the Children of Alcoholics*. New York: Teachers College Press, 1982. By drawing on the experience of a national model program, this publication shows how children of alcoholics can be helped by professionals with whom they have regular contact.

Dulfano, Celia. *Families, Alcoholism, and Recovery—Ten Stories*. Center City, MN: Hazelden Foundation, 1982. Case studies of families' interactions with an alcoholic member that serve as useful guides for counselors of alcoholics and family members.

Elkin, Michael. *Families Under the Influence: Changing Alcoholic Patterns*, New York: W. W. Norton, 1984.

Elkind, D. *The Hurried Child*. Reading, MA: Addison-Wesley, 1982.

Focus on Alcohol and Drug Issues (2), (3), (4) 1983. This series of three magazine issues focusing on the chemically dependent family is available from U.S. Journal of Drug and Alcohol Dependence, Inc., 1721 Blount Road, Suite 1, Pompano Beach, FL 33069.

Ford, Betty, and Chase, Chris. *Betty: A Glad Awakening*. New York: Doubleday, 1986.

Fox, Ruth. *The Effects of Alcoholism on Children*. Reprinted from the Proceedings of the V International Congress on Psychotherapy. Available through National Council on Alcoholism, 733 Third Avenue, New York, NY 10020.

Gleason Milgram, Gail. *What, When, and How To Talk to Children About Alcohol and Other Drugs: A Guide for Parents*. Center City, MN: Hazelden Foundation.

Goodwin, Donald, M. D. *Is Alcoholism Hereditary?* New York: Oxford University Press, 1976. A clear, well-written text on inherited and environmental factors of familial alcoholism.

Goodwin, D. W. "The Genetics of Alcoholism: A State-of-the Art Review." *Alcohol Health and Research World* 2, no. 3 (1978): 2-12.

Gravitz, Herbert L., and Bowden, Julie D. *Guide to Recovery. A Book for Adult Children of Alcoholics.* Holmes Beach, FL: Learning Publications, 1985.

Hastings, J. M. *An Elephant in the Living Room: The Children's Book.* Minneapolis: CompCare Publications, 1983.

Hastings, J. M., and Typpo, M. H. *An Elephant in the Living Room: A Guide for Working with Children of Alcoholics.* Minneapolis: CompCare Publications, 1983.

Health Communications. *Changing Legacies: Growing Up in an Alcoholic Home.* Pompano Beach, FL: Health Communications, 1984.

Holbrooke, Blythe. *Baby Teeth.* New York: Simon & Schuster, 1986.

Lawson, Gary; Peterson, James S.; and Lawson, Ann. *Alcoholism and the Family. A Guide to Treatment and Prevention.* Rockville, MD: Aspen Systems, 1983.

Lewis, David C., and Williams, Carol N. *Providing Care for Children of Alcoholics.* Pompano Beach, FL: Health Communications, 1986.

Luks, Allan. *Will America Sober Up?* Boston: Beacon Press, 1983. A call for a national campaign to help Americans drink moderately and achieve better health.

——, ed. *The Rights of Alcoholics and Their Families.* New York: Alcoholism Council of Greater New York, New York City Affiliate, National Council on Alcoholism, 1976.

McConnel, Patty. *A Workbook for Healing: Adult Children of Alcoholics.* San Francisco: Harper & Row, 1986.

Marlin, Emily. *Hope: New Choices and Recovery Strategies for Adult Children of Alcoholics.* New York: Harper & Row, 1987.

Maxwell, Ruth. *The Booze Battle.* New York: Ballantine Books, 1976. A book for spouses, employers, families, and friends of alcoholics.

Melton, Carol S. *Family Business: Recovery for Adult Children of Alcoholics.* Los Angeles: Ergo Media, 1987.

Meryman, Richard. *Broken Promises, Mended Dreams.* Boston: Little, Brown, 1984. The story of life with an alcoholic mother and the effects of the disease and the recovery process on the entire family.

Middelton-Moz, Jane, and Lorie Dwinell. *After the Tears: Multigenerational Grief in Alcoholic Families.* Pompano Beach, FL: Health Communications, 1986.

Morehouse, E. "Assessing and Motivating Adolescents Who Abuse Alcohol." *Social Work Treatment of Alcohol Problems,* Treatment Series, Vol. 5. Rutgers Center for Alcohol Studies. New Brunswick, NJ: Lexington Press, 1983.

———. *Preventing Alcohol Problems through a Student Assistance Program.* Rockville, MD: National Institute on Alcohol Abuse and Alcoholism, 1984.

———. "Working in the Schools with Children of Alcoholic Parents." *Health and Social Work* 4, no. 4 (1979).

Morrison, Toni. *The Bluest Eye.* New York: Pocket Books, Simon & Schuster, 1972.

National Association of State Alcohol and Drug Abuse Directors. *Resource Directory of National Alcohol-Related Associations, Agencies and Organizations.* Washington, DC: the Association, 1985.

National Institute on Alcohol Abuse and Alcoholism. *Biological/Genetic Factors in Alcoholism.* Research Monograph 9. Rockville, MD: Alcohol, Drug Abuse and Mental Health Administration, U.S. Department of Health and Human Services, 1983. The text consists of significant research findings on various topics related to alcohol abuse and alcoholism.

———. "Preventing Alcohol-Related Birth Defects." *Alcohol Health and Research World.* Special Focus Issue (Fall 1985).

———. *Services for Children of Alcoholics.* Research Monograph 4. Rockville, MD: Alcohol, Drug Abuse and Mental Health Administration, U.S. Department of Health and Human Services, 1979. Monograph of symposium and papers submitted by participants assessing critical policy issues of identification, intervention, treatment, and prevention, as well as recommendations (free).

———. *Sixth Special Report to the U.S. Congress on Alcohol and Health.* Rockville, MD: Alcohol, Drug Abuse and Mental Health Administration, U.S. Department of Health and Human Services, 1987.

National Institute on Drug Abuse. *Highlights of the 1985 National Household Survey on Drug Abuse.* Rockville, MD.: U.S. Department of Health and Human Services, 1986.

O'Gorman, Patricia H., and Oliver-Diaz, Philip. *Breaking the Cycle of Addiction: A Parent's Guide to Raising Healthy Kids.* Pompano Beach, FL: Health Communications, 1987.

O'Gorman, P., and Ross, R. A. "Children of Alcoholics in the Juvenile Justice System." *Alcohol Health and Research World* (Summer 1984): 43-45.

Porterfield, Kay Marie. *Coping with an Alcoholic Parent.* New York: Rosen Publishing Group, 1985.

———. *Familiar Strangers.* Center City, MN: Hazelden Foundation, 1984.

Rachel, V. *Family Secrets: Life Stories of Adult Children of Alcoholics*. San Francisco: Harper & Row, 1987.

Richards, T. *"Working with Children of an Alcoholic Mother."* Alcohol Health and Research World 3, no. 3 (1979): 22-25.

Robe, Lucy Barry. *Just So It's Healthy*. Minneapolis: CompCare Publications, 1982.

Robinson, Bryan E. *Working with Children of Alcoholics*. Lexington, MA: D. C. Heath, 1989.

Russell, Marcia; Henderson, Cynthia; and Blume, Sheila. *Children of Alcoholics: A Review of the Literature*. New York: Children of Alcoholics Foundation, 1985. A comprehensive review of the literature that looks critically at the entire breadth of recent research relevant to children of alcoholics and is intended to give the interested scientist/professional both an overview and a synthesis of current knowledge to identify important leads, and to point out gaps in knowledge. The seven sections of the *Review* are: Genetic Factors in Alcoholism; Genetically Influenced Characteristics Related to Alcohol; Germ Cell and In Utero Effects of Parental Alcohol Use on the Child; Familial Transmission of Psychiatric and Physical Disorders Associated with Alcoholism; Family Studies in Alcoholism; Prevention and Treatment; Ethics and Public Policy Issues. Available from Children of Alcoholics Foundation (free).

Ryerson, Eric. *When Your Parent Drinks Too Much: A Book for Teenagers*. New York: Facts on File, 1985.

Scales, Cynthia G. *Potato Chips for Breakfast*. Rockaway, NJ: Quotidian Press, 1986.

Seixas, Judith. *Living with a Parent Who Drinks Too Much*. New York: Greenwillow Books, 1979.

Seixas, J. S., and Youcha, G. *Children of Alcoholism: A Survivor's Manual*. New York: Crown, 1985. A moving portrait that provides valuable advice to adult children of alcoholics about how to survive and how to recover, plus useful information for their families, friends, associates, and employers.

Smith, Ann. *Grandchildren of Alcoholics*. Pompano Beach, FL: Health Communications, 1988.

Somers, Suzanne. *Keeping Secrets*. New York: Warner Books, 1988.

Stanek, Muriel. *Don't Hurt Me, Mama*. Niles, IL: Albert Whitman, 1983.

Straus, M. A.; Gelles, R. J.; and Steinmetz, S. K. *Behind Closed Doors: Violence in the American Family*. New York: Doubleday, 1980.

Subby, Robert. *Lost in the Shuffle: The Co-Dependent Reality*. Pompano Beach, FL: Health Communications, 1987.

Thompson, C., and Rudolph, L. *Counseling Children*. Monterey, CA: Brooks/ Cole Publishing Co., 1983.

Wegscheider, Don. *If Only My Family Understood Me*. Minneapolis: CompCare Publications, 1979.

Wegscheider, Sharon. *Another Chance, Hope and Health for the Alcoholic Family*. Palo Alto, CA: Science & Behavior Books, 1981. Describes experiences of alcoholic families, roles family members assume, and discusses treatment methods to combat the disease.

_____. "Children of Alcoholics Caught in a Family Trap." *Focus on Alcohol and Drug Issues* 2, no. 8 (1979).

_____. *The Family Trap*. Minneapolis: Nurturing Networks, 1979.

_____. *A Second Chance*. Palo Alto, CA: Science & Behavior Books, 1980.

Wegscheider-Cruse, Sharon. *Choicemaking*. Pompano Beach, FL: Health Communications, 1985.

West, Louis Jolyon, ed. *Alcoholism and Related Problems: Issues for the American Public*. Englewood Cliffs, NJ: Prentice-Hall, American Assembly, 1984.

Whitfield, Charles L. *Healing the Child Within: Discovery and Rediscovery for Adult Children of Dysfunctional Families*. Pompano Beach, FL: Health Communications, 1987.

_____. *Guidelines for Support Groups: Adult Children of Alcoholics and Others Who Identify*. Pompano Beach, FL: Health Communications, 1986.

Woititz, Janet G. *Adult Children of Alcoholics*. Pompano Beach, FL: Health Communications, 1983.

_____. "Guidelines for Support Groups." Pompano Beach, FL: Health Communications, 1986.

_____. *Marriage on the Rocks*. Pompano Beach, FL: Health Communications, 1983.

Woodside, Migs. *Children of Alcoholics*. New York: New York State Division of Alcoholism and Alcohol Abuse, Children of Alcoholics Foundation, 1982.

Zimberg, Sheldon; Wallace, John; and Blume, Sheila, eds. *Practical Approaches to Alcoholism Psychotherapy*, 2d ed. New York and London: Plenum Press, 1985.

CompCare Publications
21415 Annapolis Lane
Minneapolis, MN 55441
800-328-3330

Health Communications, Inc.
1721 Blount Road, Suite #1
Pompano Beach, FL 33069
305-979-5408

CASPAR Alcohol Education Program
226 Highland Avenue
Somerville, MA 02143

Johnson Institute
510 First Avenue North
Minneapolis, MN 55403
612-341-0435

Hazelden Foundation
Educational Materials
Box 176
Center City, MN 55012
800-328-9000

Learn Me Inc.
Children's Book Store
542 Grand Avenue
St. Paul, MN 55105
612-291-7888

Other

Children Are People Support Group Manual & Support Group Kit, 1982, Rev. ed., 1985. Children Are People, 493 Selby Avenue, St. Paul, MN 55102.

Clarke, Jean Illsley. *Who—Me Lead a Group?* Minneapolis: Winston Press, 1984.

"Stamp Game." Mac Publishing, Division of Claudja, Inc., 5005 East 39th Avenue, Denver, CO 80207 (303-331-0148).

For Students

Films, Videos

All Bottled Up. 11 min. Dynamics of growing up with alcoholic parent. Suggests ways to take care of yourself. For teenagers and concerned adults. Excellent animation.

Bitter Wind. 30 min. 1973. Depicts the attempts of a son to reunite his alcoholic Navajo family. Available from Department of Audio-Visual Communications, Brigham Young University, Provo, UT 84601.

Children of Denial. 28 min. 1983. Features Claudia Black speaking about youngsters, adolescents, and adults as children of alcoholics. Three basic tenets rule the lives of these children: don't talk, don't trust, don't feel. Available from ACT, P. O. Box 8536, Newport Beach, CA 92660.

Drinking Parents. 10 min. 1982. Through conversations with a recovered alcoholic mother and her teenage daughter, their feelings and the frustrations of their situation are discussed from both viewpoints. The primary objective of this film is to emphasize that young people with alcoholic parents can get help from community resources and not remain isolated. Available from MTI Teleprograms, Inc., 4825 North Scoot Street, Suite 23, Schiller Park, IL 60176.

How Do You Tell? 35 min. VHS and 16mm. Coronet Films, 108 Wilmot Road, Deerfield, IL 60015.

Lots of Kids Like Us. 28 min. VHS. Designed to help children deal with problems of living in an alcoholic home. Factual information about impact on whole family. With Discussion Guide.

Soft Is the Heart of a Child. VHS. Powerful story of family threatened by alcoholism, with focus on children. How school counselor and teachers help them resolve to help themselves. For children and adults.

Story About Feelings. 10 min. 16mm. Helps children understand the role that feelings play, which can give them the strength to say no. Ten years and under. Johnson Institute.

The Wizard of No. 16mm. Animated. A magical wizard teaches how to say no to harmful influences and how to protect yourself.

Printed Matter

Al-Anon Family Group. *Alateen—Hope for Children of Alcoholics.* New York: Al-Anon Family Group Headquarters, 1973.

———. *What's "Drunk," Mama?* New York: Al-Anon Family Group Headquarters, 1977.

———. *Youth and the Alcoholic Parent.* New York: Al-Anon Family Group Headquarters, 1985.

Alibrandi, Tom. *Young Alcoholics.* Minneapolis: CompCare Publications, 1978.

Balcerzak, Ann M. *Familiar Strangers.* Center City, MN: Hazelden Foundation, 1984.

———. *Hope for Young People with Alcoholic Parents.* Center City, MN: Hazelden Foundation, 1981.

Black, Claudia. *My Dad Loves Me, My Dad Has a Disease.* Newport Beach, CA: ACT, 1979.

Brooks, Cathleen. *The Secret Everyone Knows*. San Diego, CA: Operation Cork, 1981.

Children Are People, Inc. *Children Are People Support Group Manual*. Rev. ed. St. Paul, MN: CAP, 1985.

Dolmetsch, Paul, and Mauricette, Gail, eds. *Teens Talk About Alcohol and Alcoholism*. Garden City, NY: Doubleday, 1987.

Duggan, Maureen H. *Mommy Doesn't Live Here Anymore*. Weaverville, NC: Bonnie Brae Publications, 1987.

Fettig, Art. *The Three Robots Learn About Drugs*. Battle Creek, MI: Growth Unlimited, 1987.

Figueroa, Ronny. *Pablito's Secret/El Secreto DePablito*. Hollywood, FL: Health Communications, 1984.

Fox, Paula. *The Moonlight Man*. New York: Bradbury Press, 1986.

Hammond, Mary, and Chestnut, Lynnann. *My Mom Doesn't Look Like an Alcoholic*. Pompano Beach, FL: Health Communications, 1984.

Hastings, Jill M., and Typpo, Marian H. *An Elephant in the Living Room*. Minneapolis: CompCare Publications, 1984.

Hazelden Foundation. *Learn About Children of Alcoholics*. Center City, MN: the Foundation, 1985.

_____. *Learn About Youth and Drug Addiction*. Center City, MN: the Foundation, 1985.

Heckler, JanEllen. *A Fragile Peace*. New York: G. P. Putnam's Sons, 1986.

Hornick-Beer, Edith Lynn. *A Teenager's Guide to Living with an Alcoholic Parent*. Center City, MN: Hazelden Educational Materials, 1984.

Hyde, Margaret D. *Alcohol: Uses and Abuses*. Hillside, NJ: Enslow, 1988.

Jance, Judith A. *Welcome Home*. Edmonds, WA: Franklin Press, 1986.

Johnson Institute. *Story of Feelings:* Colorbook, workbook for the film *Story of Feelings*. Minneapolis: the Institute.

Kenny, Kevin, and Krull, Helen. *Sometimes My Mom Drinks Too Much*. Milwaukee, WI: Raintree, 1980.

Leite, E., and Espeland, P. *Different Like Me, A Book for Teens Who Worry About Their Parents' Use of Alcohol/Drugs*. Minneapolis: Johnson Institute, 1987.

LeShan, Eda. *What Makes Me Feel This Way? Growing Up with Human Emotions.* New York: Collier Books, 1972.

Melquist, Elaine L. *Pepper.* New York: National Council on Alcoholism, 1974.

Mills, Dixie, and Deutch, Charles. *Happy Hill Farm.* Somerville, MA: Caspar Alcohol Education Program, 226 Highland Avenue. ($.50)

Morrison, Toni. *The Bluest Eye.* New York: Pocket Books, Simon & Schuster, 1972.

Palmer, Pat. *Liking Myself.* Assertiveness for Young People. (ages 5-9). Palo Alto, CA: Impact Publications, 1977.

_____. *The Mouse, the Monster and Me.* Assertiveness for Young People (ages 8-12). Palo Alto, CA: Impact Publications, 1977.

Porterfield, Kay Marie. *Coping with an Alcoholic Parent.* New York: Rosen Publishing Group, 1985.

Robe, Lucy Barry. *Haunted Inheritance.* Minneapolis: CompCare Publications, 1980.

Ryerson, Eric. *When Your Parent Drinks Too Much: A Book for Teenagers.* New York: Facts on File, 1985.

_____. *Living with an Alcoholic Parent.* New York: Greenwillow Books, 1979.

Seixas, Judith S. *Alcohol: What It Is, What It Does.* New York: Greenwillow Books, 1979.

_____. *Drugs, What They Are, What They Do.* New York: Greenwillow Books, 1987.

_____. *Living with a Parent Who Drinks Too Much.* New York: Greenwillow Books, 1979.

Snyder, Anne. *Kids and Drinking.* Minneapolis: CompCare Publications, 1979.

What Every Kid Should Know about Alcohol. Channing L. Bete Co., 1982.

Wheat, Patte. *You're Not Alone.* Chicago: National Committee for Prevention of Child Abuse, 1985.

Wilt, Joy. *You're All Right, A Children's Book About Human Similarities.* Waco, TX: Word, 1979.

_____. *You're One-of-a Kind, A Children's Book About Human Uniqueness.* Waco, TX: Word, 1979.

B. NATIONAL AND STATE ORGANIZATIONS

Addiction Research Foundation
33 Russell Street
Toronto, Ontario, Canada
M55 2S1
416-595-6000

Adult Children of Alcoholics
6381 Hollywood Boulevard
Suite 685
Hollywood, CA 90028
213-464-4423

Al-Anon/Alateen Family Group
   Headquarters, Inc.
P.O. Box 862
Midtown Station
New York, NY 10018-0862
212-302-7240

Alcoholics Anonymous (AA)
P.O. Box 459
Grand Central Station
New York, NY 10163-1100
212-686-1100

Alcoholics Anonymous Intergroup
175 Fifth Avenue, Suite 219
New York, NY 10010

American Humane Association
Children's Division
P.O. Box 1266
Denver, CO 80201
303-695-0811

Big Brothers/Big Sisters of America
117 South 17th Street
Suite 1200
Philadelphia, PA 19103

Child Care Information Center
532 Settlers Landing Road
P.O. Box 548
Hampton, VA 23669
804-722-4495

Child Welfare League of America,
   Inc.
67 Irving Place
New York, NY 10003
212-254-7410

Children of Alcoholics
The New Jersey Task Force
P.O. Box 190
Rutherford, NJ 07070
201-460-7912

Children of Alcoholics Foundation,
   Inc.
200 Park Avenue, 31st floor
New York, NY 10166
212-949-1404

Children Are People, Inc.
493 Selby Avenue
St. Paul, MN 55102
612-227-4031

COA Review
The Newsletter About Children
   of Alcoholics
P.O. Box 190
Rutherford, NJ 07070
201-460-7912

Community Intervention, Inc.
220 South Tenth Street
Minneapolis, MN 55403
612-332-6537

Emotions Anonymous
P.O. Box 4245
St. Paul, MN 55104
612-647-9712

Families Anonymous
P.O. Box 344
Torrance, CA 90501

Institute on Black Chemical Abuse
2614 Nicollet Avenue
Minneapolis, MN 55408
612-871-7878

National Association
  for Children of Alcoholics
31706 Coast Highway, Suite 201
South Laguna, CA 92677
714-499-3889

National Association of Native
  American Children of Alcoholics
P.O. Box 3364
Seattle, WA 98114
206-324-9360

National Black Alcoholism Council,
  Inc.
417 S. Dearborn Street, Suite 1000
Chicago, IL 60605
312-663-5780

National Clearinghouse for Alcohol
  Information
P.O. Box 2345
Rockville, MD 20852
301-468-2600

National Council on Alcoholism
12 West 21st Street
New York, NY 10010
212-206-6770

National Council on Alcoholism
Michigan Division
2875 Northwind, Suite 225
E. Lansing, MI 48823

National Institute on Alcohol Abuse
  and Alcoholism
5600 Fishers Lane
Rockville, MD 20857
301-443-2403

New York State Coalition for the
  Children of Alcoholic Families
P.O. Box 9
Hempstead, NY 11550

Operation Cork
8939 Villa LaJolla Drive
San Diego, CA 92037

Other Victims of Alcoholism, Inc.
P.O. Box 921
Radio City Station
New York, NY 10019
212-247-8087

Parental Stress Service, Inc.
154 Santa Clara Avenue
Oakland, CA 95610
415-841-1750

Parents Anonymous
National Office
7120 Franklin Avenue
Los Angeles, CA 90046
1-800-371-3501

Parents Anonymous
22330 Hawthorne Boulevard
Suite 208
Torrance, CA 90505

Public Affairs Pamphlets
381 Park Avenue South
New York, NY 10016

Rutgers Center of Alcohol Studies
P.O. Box 969
Piscataway, NJ 08854
201-932-2190

Survivors Network
18653 Ventura Boulevard, #143
Tarzana, CA 91356

U.S. National Institute of Alcohol
   Abuse & Alcoholism
P.O. Box 2345
Rockville, MD 20852

Call each number listed in the yellow pages under "Alcoholism" or "Alcoholism Information and Treatment Centers," and in the white pages listed under "Alcoholics" and "National Council on Alcoholism." Ask for information about chemical dependence.

C. STUDENT RISK FACTORS*

Students who *may* be at risk of failure include those who—

1. are poor and lack necessities of life (food, clothing, shelter)
2. feel they do not ''belong'' at the school
3. are very quiet/withdrawn
4. exhibit disruptive behavior and rebellious attitudes
5. abuse drugs and alcohol
6. have an excessively stressful or unstable home life
7. have low self-esteem
8. are unable to tolerate structured activities
9. are loners or are not accepted by their peers
10. are way behind in their schoolwork
11. are below the expected grade level for their age
12. have poor grades or low achievement test scores
13. are new to the culture and the country
14. have a home language other than English and are limited English proficient
15. fail to learn to read
16. exhibit low ability
17. are gifted and talented but are bored with school
18. are more mobile than other students (move around a lot)
19. want to get married while still in school
20. have parents with very little education
21. have siblings or parents who have been dropouts
22. fail to see the relevance of education to later life experiences or success
23. have poor social adjustment

*From paper by Richard L. Towers delivered at the University of Maryland on July 7, 1988.

24. live away from their parents' home

25. have poor home or school communications

26. are frequently absent or tardy

27. have chronic health problems, including handicapping conditions

28. are parents

29. do not like school or their teachers

30. perceive school to be uninterested in them

31. perceive school discipline as unfair and ineffective

32. have difficulty relating to authority figures or structured situations

33. are abused and/or neglected

34. have parents and/or siblings who abuse drugs and/or alcohol.

NOTES

Chapter 1. Introduction

1. Lawrence Metzger, *From Denial to Recovery* (San Francisco: Jossey-Bass, 1988), 190–91.
2. National Institute on Alcohol Abuse and Alcoholism, *Fourth Special Report to the U.S. Congress on Alcohol and Health from the Secretary of Health and Human Services, January 1981*, edited by J. R. De Luca. DHHS Pub. No. (ADM) 81–1080 (Washington, DC: Government Printing Office, 1981).
3. Metzger, *From Denial to Recovery*, 8–12.
4. National Institute on Alcohol Abuse and Alcoholism, *Fourth Special Report to the U.S. Congress on Alcohol and Health.*
5. Lloyd D. Johnston and others, *Monitoring the Future: A Continuing Study of the Lifestyles and Values of Youths*, NIDA (Washington, DC: Government Printing Office, 1989).
5a. Karol Kumpfer, "Promising Prevention Strategies for Children of Substance Abusers," *OSAP High-Risk Youth Update*, February 1989, 1.

Chapter 2. The Risks

6. Marion H. Typpo and Jill M. Hastings, *An Elephant in the Living Room, A Leader's Guide for Helping Children of Alcoholics* (Minneapolis: CompCare Publishers, 1984), 2.
7. Ibid., 3.
8. Ibid.
9. Ibid.
10. Ibid., 4.
11. Ibid., 3.
12. Ibid., 3–4.
13. Metzger, *From Denial to Recovery*, 189–90.
14. Ibid.
15. Ibid.
16. Ibid.
17. Ibid., 190.
18. Ibid.
19. Ellen R. Morehouse and Claire M. Scola, *Children of Alcoholics: Meeting the Needs of the Young COA in the School Setting* (South Laguna,

CA: The National Association for Children of Alcoholics, 1986), 3; Metzger, *From Denial to Recovery*, 191–205.

20. Metzger, *From Denial to Recovery*, 193.
21. Morehouse and Scola, *Children of Alcoholics*, 4.
22. Metzger, *From Denial to Recovery*, 197.
23. Morehouse and Scola, *Children of Alcoholics*, 4.
24. Metzger, *From Denial to Recovery*, 198–200.
25. *Support Group Training Manual* (St. Paul, MN: Children Are People, 1985), 8.
26. Ibid.
27. Metzger, *From Denial to Recovery*, 198–200.
28. *Support Group Training Manual*, 9.
29. Ibid.
30. Metzger, *From Denial to Recovery*, 202.
31. Ibid.
32. Morehouse and Scola, *Children of Alcoholics*, 3.
33. Cited in Metzger, *From Denial to Recovery*, 202.
34. Ibid., 203.
35. Ibid.
36. Ibid.
37. *Support Group Training Manual*, 9.
38. Morehouse and Scola, *Children of Alcoholics*, 7.
39. Metzger, *From Denial to Recovery*, 189–92, 206–7.
40. Metzger, *From Denial to Recovery*, 206–7.

Chapter 3. How Schools Are Affected

41. Charles L. Whitfield, M.D., "Children of Alcoholics: Treatment Issues," *State Medical Journal* 29, no. 6 (1980): 89–91.
42. Ibid.
43. Linda A. Bennett and others, "Problems Among School-Age Children of Alcoholic Parents," *DATA, Brown University Digest of Addiction Theory and Application*, July 1988, 9–11.
44. Ibid.
45. David Wilmes, "Physical and Psychological Effects on Children of Parental Alcoholism." (Mimeo.)
46. Ibid.
47. Ibid.
48. Ibid.
49. Whitfield, "Children of Alcoholics: Treatment Issues."

50. Ibid.

51. Wilmes, "Physical and Psychological Effects on Children of Parental Alcoholism."

52. Ibid.

53. Ibid.

54. Claudia Black, *It Will Never Happen to Me* (Denver: M.A.C. Printing and Publications, 1981); Sharon Wegscheider, "Children of Alcoholics Caught in Family Trap," *Focus on Alcohol and Drug Issues* 2 (May-June 1979).

55. Margaret Cork, *The Forgotten Child* (Toronto: Paper Jacks, 1969), 61.

Chapter 4. A Family Disease

56. Kathleen Whalen Fitzgerald, *Alcoholism, the Genetic Inheritance* (New York: Doubleday, 1988), XII.

57. *The Family Enablers*, rev. ed. (Minneapolis: The Johnson Institute, 1987), 3.

58. Fitzgerald, *Alcoholism, the Genetic Inheritance*, XII.

59. Ibid.

60. Cited in Metzger, *From Denial to Recovery*, 4–5.

61. Ibid., 10–11.

62. *The Family Enablers*, 3–11.

63. Ibid., 3.

64. Cited in Sandy Rovner, "Helping Families Face the Facts," *Washington Post Health Section*, 27 December 1988, 16.

65. Sharon Wegscheider, *Another Chance: Hope and Health for the Alcoholic Family* (Palo Alto, CA: Science & Behavior Books, 1981).

66. Black, *It Will Never Happen to Me*, 59.

67. Cited in Gary G. Forrest, *How to Cope with a Teenage Drinker* (New York: Ballantine Books, 1983), 40–42.

68. Black, *It Will Never Happen to Me*, 31–49.

69. Don Colburn, "Undoing the Damage," *Washington Post Health Section*, 27 December 1988, 6–9.

70. Paul Berg, "Teens in Trouble," *Washington Post Health Section*, 27 December 1988, 15.

71. Cited in Colburn, "Undoing the Damage," 9.

72. Ibid.

73. Robert J. Ackerman, *Children of Alcoholics, A Guide for Parents, Educators, and Therapists*, 2d ed. (New York: Simon & Schuster, 1983), 49–52.

74. Ibid.
75. Morehouse and Scola, *Children of Alcoholics,* 3–5; Ackerman, *Children of Alcoholics,* 55–58.

Chapter 5. What Schools Can Do

76. Richard L. Towers, *How Schools Can Help Combat Student Drug and Alcohol Abuse* (Washington, DC: National Education Association, 1987).
77. Ackerman, *Children of Alcoholics,* 105–6.
78. Ibid.
79. Bennett and others, "Problems Among School-Age Children of Alcoholic Parents," 9; "Heredity and Drinking: How Strong Is the Link?" *Newsweek,* 18 January 1980, 66–67.
80. Ackerman, *Children of Alcoholics,* 98–103.
81. Ibid., 99.
82. Morehouse and Scola, *Children of Alcoholics,* 13.
83. Ibid.
84. Ibid., 14.
85. *Support Group Training Manual,* 12–13.
86. Ibid., 6, 10.
87. Morehouse and Scola, *Children of Alcoholics,* 18.
88. *Support Group Training Manual,* 6, 10.
89. Cited in Ibid., 52.
90. Ibid., 54.
91. "When and Where" (New York: Alcoholics Anonymous World Services, 1988).
92. Morehouse and Scola, *Children of Alcoholics,* 16.
93. Typpo and Hastings, *An Elephant in the Living Room,* 74–75.
94. Kathryn J. Brake, "Counseling Young Children of Alcoholics," *Elementary School Guidane and Counseling* (December 1988): 107.
95. Ibid., 108.
96. Amy Burwick and others, "Helping Children Deal with Alcoholism in Their Families," *Elementary School Guidance and Counseling* (28 December 1988): 112–17.
97. Morehouse and Scola, *Children of Alcoholics,* 20.
98. Gary L. Anderson, "Solving Alcohol/Drug Problems in Your School, Why Student Assistance Programs Work (Minneapolis: Johnson Institute, 1988), 13.
99. Albert F. Borris, "Three Organizational Models," *Student Assistance*

Journal (November/December 1988): 31–33.

100. Cynthia Tower, *How Schools Can Help Combat Child Abuse and Neglect*, 2d ed. (Washington, DC: National Education Association, 1987).

101. Lynn Jacob and Donna Marmer, "Identifying and Working with Children from Chemically Dependent Families." (Mimeo., n.d.)

102. "If a Child from an Alcoholic Home Comes to You" (Rockville, MD: National Clearinghouse on Alcohol Information.) (Mimeo., n.d.)

103. Metzger, *From Denial to Recovery*, 200–205.

104. Towers, *How Schools Can Help Combat Student Drug and Alcohol Abuse,* 147–50.

NEA Policy on
Student Stress

Resolution C-12. Student Stress

The National Education Association believes that there are increasing mental, emotional, and environmental pressures upon the children and youth of this nation. These pressures—resulting in increased drug and alcohol abuse, violence, vandalism, dropping out of school, and suicide among children and youth—speak clearly to the waste of human potential.

The Association urges its local and state affiliates to support appropriately accredited and licensed mental health and aftercare programs for students and to provide staff development workshops for personnel in direct contact with these students.

The Association further urges local and state affiliates to seek legislative support and publicity for these programs. (80, 89)